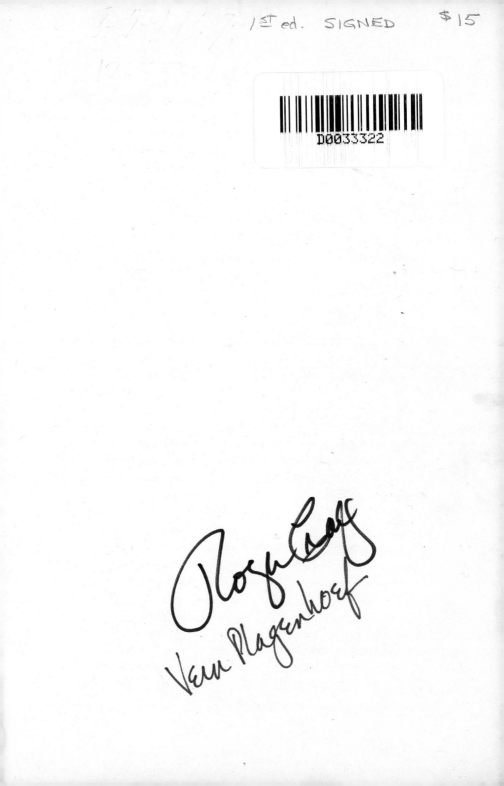

INSIDE PITCH

Roger Craig's
'84
Tiger Journal

With Vern Plagenhoef

WM. B. EERDMANS PUBLISHING CO.
255 JEFFERSON AVE. S.E. / GRAND RAPIDS, MICHIGAN 49503

For Carolyn

Copyright © 1984 by William B. Eerdmans Publishing Company
255 Jefferson Ave. S.E., Grand Rapids, Mich. 49503

ISBN 0-8028-7048-1

COVER PHOTO CREDITS
Background photo courtesy the *Ann Arbor News,* Jack Stubbs; upper left inset courtesy the Detroit Tigers, Rankin; upper right courtesy the Detroit Tigers, Clifton Boutelle; lower right courtesy the Detroit Tigers, Joe Arcure.

FOREWORD

I N 1984, at the age of fifty-four, Roger Craig delivered a World Championship from the mound of the Detroit Tigers. His pitching staff—Jack Morris, Dan Petry, Milt Wilcox, Juan Berenguer, Willie Hernandez, Aurelio Lopez, Dave Rozema, Doug Bair, and Bill Scherrer—fired the Tigers into history. This team had the best start in Tiger history, 9-0; the best thirty-game start in major league history, 26-4; the best forty-game start in major league history, 35-5; an American League record for most consecutive road victories, 17; a club record for victories, 104; and the distinction of being the third team in major league history, and the first since the 1927 New York Yankees, to hold first place from Opening Day to the final day of the season.

The Tigers captured the league earned run championship with a mark of 3.49. They were the only club to finish among the top five in that category each of the past four years. They also won the ERA distinction in 1982 under the guidance of Craig. "Roger can be very proud to have won the earned run title with a mark that low in a league with the designated hitter and in a ballpark [Tiger Stadium] where pitchers are prone to give up a lot of runs," praised Tiger manager Sparky Anderson.

The statistics on Craig's staff were dramatic in their consistency. Willie Hernandez, a strong candidate for both the Most Valuable Player and Cy Young awards, saved thirty-two games in thirty-three save opportunities. That remarkable feat was nearly matched by Aurelio Lopez, who won ten of eleven decisions and tacked on fourteen saves. The two combined for a 19-4 won-lost record and forty-six saves. Jack Morris, Dan Petry, and Milt Wilcox combined for fifty-four victories, even though they recorded only sixteen complete games. Wilcox, who has been plagued by arm problems in recent seasons, had no complete games, but won seventeen because Craig kept him healthy the entire season. "All the credit goes to Roger," said Wilcox. "He has been a teacher and a drill sergeant. I've learned to pitch with Roger. He has taught me a great assortment of pitches and has taught me the value of making constant adjustments during the course of a season and a career."

Few pitchers have experienced as much success and failure as Craig. Roger pitched for four World Series teams—the 1955 and 1956 Brooklyn Dodgers, the 1959 Los Angeles Dodgers, and the 1964 St. Louis Cardinals. He also was the ace of the staff for Casey Stengel's Amazin' Mets in 1962-63, when he lost a total of forty-six games, including eighteen in a row in 1963. Craig pitched in eleven shutout losses that season, five of which were 1-0. "I know the ups and downs of major league baseball," said Craig. "Losing was a tremendous influence in shaping my pitching philosophy. I learned the value of being competitive, regardless of the circumstances. I learned the value of positive thinking and the power of self-esteem."

Craig has preached that philosophy in five seasons as Anderson's chief assistant and confidant. To his pitchers, Craig was a teacher and a friend, a sounding board and an architect, an authority figure who made his pupils earn their stripes. He gave his pitchers the knowledge he accumulated in thirty-five years of professional baseball. "In the old days, players were constantly criticized," said Craig. "Today, players receive pats on the back. There's really no other way to handle people armed with long-term, guaranteed contracts."

Pitching personalities are like a variety pack of breakfast cereals. Petry, for instance, enjoys visits to the mound. Morris, however, does not like Anderson, Craig, or anyone else to visit him, which he feels disturbs his concentration. Jack, who provided one of the season's top thrills by pitching a no-hit game, also presented Craig with his biggest challenge. The petulant Morris was prone to temper tantrums. Mid-season he went into a period of silence for six weeks, during which he refused to talk to the media. "I had to approach Jack in the proper manner or I might have lost him for the season," stated Craig. Morris eventually ended his period of silence in late August.

Another challenge for Craig was Hernandez, who had a

Roger Craig – master craftsman and capable teacher

different kind of personality. "I had to learn what made Willie tick," admitted Craig. "He was arrogant at first and he tested me by attempting to put me on the defensive. I rolled with the punches. . . . We have become close friends."

Pitching and coaching are both studies in psychology. "Gaylord Perry used to cover baseballs with vaseline and roll the ball to an opposing batter during pre-game batting practice on days he was pitching," recalled Craig. "Berenguer acts like a king on the mound. I like the way he struts around. He's a macho pitcher. Wilcox is the same way, and so is Hernandez. The way a pitcher carries himself can place pressure on a hitter. . . . If a pitcher doesn't battle and be competitive he will lose control and ultimately lose the game."

Craig has been in charge for many years, dating back to

a military stint at Fort Jackson, South Carolina, in 1953. "I was asked to pitch for two different teams," recalled Craig.

> One offered me $75 per game and the other $100 per game. I accepted the offer for $100. Every time I pitched against the team whose offer I had refused I noticed a captain sitting beside their dugout. One day after I had won a game he came up to me wearing all his medals and ribbons and said, "Private Craig, I know you've been AWOL. The next time you pitch against this club I'll send you to Korea." I went to see a colonel who was in charge of the baseball teams. I admitted I had been going AWOL, but that I lived off the post and that I had not missed any of my work assignments. The colonel said he'd handle the situation.
>
> The next time I pitched against the captain's team I beat them again and the captain wasn't in the stands. I saw the colonel later and inquired about the whereabouts of the captain. "I had a mission for him," the colonel told me. "I sent *him* to Korea!"

There is no replacement for good pitching.

*   *   *

Roger Craig has spent five years shaping his Detroit Tigers pitching staff into championship quality. He taught pitching in a manner understood by men with a broad range of personalities. This diary serves as a testament to his unbridled enthusiasm and his contagious confidence.

Craig hatched the idea for this book during spring training in Lakeland, Florida. Even then, he sensed an electrifying season. I volunteered to assist Roger in this industrious undertaking for a number of reasons. Foremost, this is a story of human relationships in the business of professional baseball. The chronology of the Detroit Tigers' remarkable 1984 season is a record of minor failures and overwhelming success. Craig's thoughts are an intimate account of one man's method of dealing with a staff of pitchers whose backgrounds ranged from Southern California to Minnesota to Panama.

Craig's taped entries seemed more and more sagacious as the season progressed. He realized everyone could empathize with his story and he recognized the importance of candor.

That's me during my military
days at Fort Jackson

My days with Stengel's Amazin' Mets
helped me cope with defeat

Petry, Morris, and Plagenhoef plot a championship season

His unfailing honesty brought a strong sense of reality to a fantasy season. It also sets him apart from many others who have attempted to capture the essence of baseball. The project was rewarding and fun. I learned a lot about baseball from Roger; he learned a lot about journalism from me. Together, we learned a lot about each other.

When we required help, it was unselfishly offered. We are indebted to Sparky Anderson and the Tiger management for not infringing upon Roger's fervent desire to present a candid Tiger's tale. We appreciate the confidence demonstrated by Eerdmans Publishing Company and Booth Newspapers, Inc., both of whom believed this diary warranted public attention. We are grateful for the tireless work of Mike Lloyd, who served the dual capacity of editor and agent. We extend heartfelt thanks to Marvin Laninga of the *Grand Rapids Press,* Jack Stubbs of the *Ann Arbor News,* Clifton Boutelle, Christopher Chagnon, and the Tigers management for their pictorial contributions.

Finally, we salute our immediate families for their under-standing of the time devoted to this project. Our wives, Carolyn and Penny, are our best friends. They patiently tolerated our desire to produce a publication of merit. My two sons, Scott and Brent, were deprived of playing time with their father. Thanks, guys. I want to dedicate my part in this book to you and mom.

Whatever else went into making this book a reality, it re-mains Roger Craig's through and through. This is a pitch from his heart.

—Vern Plagenhoef

JACK Morris returned to his boyhood home in St. Paul, Minnesota, for a nostalgic stop before his parents, Donna and Arvid Morris, move to Manistee, Michigan to a home purchased by Jack. Jack certainly must have some mixed emotions. I feel for him because I'm considering retirement at the end of this season. Baseball has been my home since 1950 and I'm not sure I want to leave.

As a kid, I used to sit outside the ballpark of the Durham (N.C.) Bulls and wait to retrieve foul balls. Those tattered balls were our ticket into the game. Of course, if the ball happened to be in real good shape we'd keep it. We couldn't afford to buy one.

The last time I set foot on the field at Bulls Park was in 1955 after I had helped the Brooklyn Dodgers win their first— and last—World Championship. That was my rookie season, and I won the pivotal fifth game of the World Series against the New York Yankees. Durham staged a big parade right down Main Street in my honor. I remember passing the Belk Legget shoe store where my father, John Thompson Craig, had worked. I pitched in an exhibition game that night against a group of major league players. The old park was filled. There were, naturally, some aspiring youngsters outside the park chasing foul balls, but the moment was bittersweet for me because my father had passed away three years earlier.

Every kid wants to salute his father for all the years of guidance and encouragement. A flashing neon sign wouldn't have served as a suitable "Thank you." Dad was gone, and that is my biggest regret.

Jack has to feel some sadness about his final night in the room that sheltered him during his developmental years, just as I feel some sadness about contemplating retirement. Sure, I'm sentimental. That's part of the beauty of Opening Day. The Tigers happen to have the type of pitchers and players who prompt me to go out on a limb and predict a championship

I'm all smiles in the uniform of the Los Angeles Dodgers

on the eve of this season. The feeling is here, the atmosphere exists, and there is a common bond that has eliminated petty jealousies.

THERE are Opening Day pitchers, and pitchers who start on Opening Day. Jack Morris probably is the best of the former—better than Don Drysdale, Jim Bunning, Bob Gibson, Sandy Koufax, Don Newcombe, and Carl Erskine. Morris just rises to the occasion. He gets his adrenaline flowing and exudes such positive thoughts that it's difficult for him to lose on Opening Day. Jack has received five consecutive Opening Day starts for the Tigers. His 8-1 victory over the Minnesota Twins here tonight represented his fourth victory. I was gratified for Jack. This was a fitting farewell to his boyhood home where he dreamed of one day pitching in the major leagues.

Jack experienced only one critical moment. In the fifth inning he struck out catcher Tim Laudner on three pitches with the tying run on third base and one out. He got Laudner

You can't ask for a better Opening Day pitcher than Jack Morris

Free agent Darrell Evans homered in his first Tiger game

on two split-fingered fastballs and a fastball that painted the black of the plate.

This was not by accident. Sparky Anderson and I meet with our pitchers and catchers before every series to discuss the strengths and weaknesses of every opposing hitter. We rely on reports provided to us by advance scout Boots Day, and we draw on our previous experience against each particular opponent. Coach Dick Tracewski also meets with our outfielders to determine defensive alignment, depending on our pitcher. For example, we don't expect the opposition to pull a hard thrower such as Juan Berenguer as much as they would Dave Rozema. I talked to Jack prior to the game about setting up his fastball, which he used to strike out Laudner. Jack has an effective rising fastball and he's not afraid to bring it inside to hitters.

Sometimes you get a clue to how well a pitcher will perform by the manner in which he warms up in the bullpen. I could tell by the fourth or fifth pitch that Jack had great snap in his wrist and a live arm action. We even decided to start his split-fingered fastball a little higher than normal in the strike zone because it was dropping dramatically—about a foot and a half. The secret to improved control is to place the fingers more on top of the ball, rather than gripping the ball deep in the fingers. Jack's slider also was working well. That gave me great satisfaction because I had convinced him during the latter stages of spring training to change his grip. He was choking the slider too much, which means the ball was set too deep in his hand. We brought the ball to the fingertips, and that resulted in more velocity and a sharper break.

Sparky and I decided to remove Jack after seven innings. We used Aurelio Lopez and Willie Hernandez for one inning apiece with our comfortable lead. This was my first look at Willie, and I liked what I saw.

I had been badgering Sparky about our need for a left-handed pitcher. But I hadn't had much input in the decision to acquire Hernandez. Ray Shore (a Phillies scout who had worked for the Reds when Sparky managed there) had talked to Sparky and me several times and expressed an interest in Glenn Wilson and John Wockenfuss. The trade had its foundation late in 1983. Shore followed our club extensively at that time. We really didn't know what we were getting in Hernandez, but everyone knew we needed a left-handed pitcher. Willie has three fine pitches—fastball, slider, and screwball—and seems to have command of all three. We'll have to wait and see.

Jack will be coming back with only three days' rest on national television in Chicago against the White Sox, last year's West Division champs. So he was not upset with our decision. His performance was self-satisfying and good enough to move Gordon Lakey, a scout for the Houston Astros, to tell me that Jack had "no-hit stuff." I wouldn't trade Jack Morris for any pitcher in either league.

TIGERS 8, TWINS 1   1 – 0

PITCHER	IP	H	R-ER	BB	SO	ERA
Morris (1-0)	7.0	5	1-1	0	8	1.29
Lopez	1.0	0	0-0	0	0	0.00
Hernandez	1.0	0	0-0	0	0	0.00

WEDNESDAY, APRIL 4   MINNEAPOLIS

O NE of the toughest jobs for a pitching coach is laying bad news on a member of his staff. Juan Berenguer was a special project of mine in 1983. He was a vagabond pitcher who won only three of twenty decisions while kicking around with the New York Mets, Kansas City Royals, and Toronto Blue Jays. The Tigers acquired him in a minor league purchase in April of 1982. Berenguer won nine of fourteen decisions for us in 1983, while recording the best earned run average among our starting pitchers. He seemed destined to be in our starting rotation this season. In fact, we had assured him he would be among the top four behind Jack Morris, Dan Petry, and Milt Wilcox. Unfortunately for Berenguer, he became a victim of the foibles of spring training. He pitched poorly his last three times out and lost his job to Dave Rozema, who opened our eyes in a four-inning simulated game here two days ago.

My main concern now is to properly guide Berenguer through difficult days. He is depressed and disappointed. Juan is a high-strung individual who was rejected by three other clubs, came to Detroit with a better arm than any scout will find beating any bushes, achieved personal satisfaction in 1983, and now has been reminded of past shortcomings.

If I have one outstanding quality it is my contagious optimistic nature. Joe Altobelli, the manager of the Baltimore Orioles, even said of me, "Roger Craig is so optimistic he could find good in a tornado." I've got to make Juan believe that if he works a little harder he can get back into the starting rotation. I'll spend a lot of time with him the next few days to build his confidence. He has to go to the bullpen and battle a little harder to reclaim his job. This is an easy time for him to mope, blame me or Sparky for his demotion, and take a step backward.

I talked to Juan at length and explained that this decision was temporary, and that he would return to starting as soon as he demonstrates better command of his breaking ball and split-fingered fastball. Juan was understandably depressed, but not angry. This is a difficult situation for anyone. Juan's livelihood is at stake. I hope he can regain his status.

Rozema, on the other hand, deserves the starting assignment on Sunday in Chicago. He pitched better in the simulated game than I've seen him pitch since he injured his left knee in a fight with the Twins on May 14, 1982. I believe Rozema could be a stabilizer on our staff. He experienced stiffness in his neck and pitching shoulder this spring, and Sparky and I considered placing him on the disabled list. That would have been a mistake. Dave was devastating Monday. Look for Rozie to have a good year. His spirits soared because of our change of plans. He was as elated as Juan was disappointed.

ONE of Dan Petry's endearing qualities is his work ethic. He will do anything you ask of him, such as adding two pitches after coming off a nineteen-victory season.

Not very many successful starting pitchers survive on two pitches as Petry did in 1983. He existed on a fastball and a slider. I felt he threw the slider too frequently and was losing command of his fastball, which is the key pitch for most twenty-five-year-old pitchers who stand six-foot-four and weigh 205 pounds. We emphasized the fastball in spring training and Petry, as always, was cooperative. He realized the addition of a curve and split-fingered fastball would prove beneficial. Today, he took his first step toward becoming a four-pitch pitcher by defeating the Minnesota Twins, 7-3. They did manage a couple of hits off his split-finger, but on natural grass, rather than the Metrodome's artificial turf, those balls would have been ground-outs. Dan also looked confident, and confidence is the only department in which he trails Jack Morris.

We lifted Dan after seven innings. Again we had a comfortable lead and he had thrown nearly one hundred pitches. We've got to get a good bead on Willie Hernandez, who thrives on work. Willie has appeared in 150 games over the past two seasons. He figures prominently in our plans.

We are entitled to expect no more than six, seven, or eight strong innings from our starters, then entrust the bullpen with the lead. We feel we have adequate depth in the bullpen with Doug Bair, Aurelio Lopez, and Hernandez. Besides, limiting the number of innings pitched by starters early in the season will pay dividends in August and September.

Dan managed a single strikeout in seven innings. This is not cause for alarm because a pitcher's arm strength generally doesn't peak until May or June. Dan doesn't really qualify as a strikeout pitcher anyway. The velocity of his fastball isn't over-powering, but the degree of movement usually results in off-center contact.

Willie retired six consecutive batters over the final two innings. I love Willie's screwball. He learned it from former Oriole Mike Cuellar following the 1982 season. That screwball dips away from right-handed hitters. It is a great equalizer if Sparky brings him in to face a left-handed hitter and the opposing manager counters with a right-handed hitter. One secret of being a good pitcher is to have a trick pitch such as the split-fingered fastball, knuckleball, or screwball.

We left for Chicago following the game. Glenn Abbott was in a mischievous mood at the Minneapolis airport where actor Sean Connery was preparing to board the same flight. Abbott attempted to persuade several players to page James Bond so we could watch Connery's reaction. No one accepted.

There has been a lot of clubhouse talk about the White Sox because they have beaten us seventeen times in twenty-four games over the previous two seasons. Many of our players still remember the day in May two years ago when LaMarr Hoyt attempted to hit Alan Trammell twice in the ninth inning, even though Hoyt had an imposing 10-3 lead. The newspapers seized on that incident. Hoyt, last year's Cy Young winner, was quoted as saying, "Who could the Tigers afford to lose more than Trammell?" The American League office investigated the matter, but took no action against Hoyt. He assured them that he didn't intentionally throw at Trammell. Most of our players don't agree, but do remember.

TIGERS 7, TWINS 3   2 − 0

PITCHER	IP	H	R-ER	BB	SO	ERA
Petry (1-0)	7.0	5	3-2	4	1	2.57
Hernandez	2.0	0	0-0	0	2	0.00

RUSTY Kuntz, a utility infielder we acquired in a minor league deal at last year's winter meetings, played Santa Claus here today. He couldn't have picked a more appropriate time. Kuntz distributed specially designed nylon undergarments to all our players, coaching staff, and trainers on a cold and blustery day. Everyone laughed because we resembled a bunch of supermen running around the clubhouse.

Rusty Kuntz kept everyone warm

The biggest chill was felt by the White Sox. We spoiled their home opener, 3-2, thanks to some gutty pitching by Milt Wilcox and Willie Hernandez. The performance was typical of Wilcox. He likes to nibble, frequently runs the count to three balls, and falls behind a lot of hitters. But he made good pitches when necessary to beat the Sox.

Wilcox always has had the ability to be a fifteen-game winner. My biggest challenge is to keep Milt healthy. He spent time on the disabled list last season with a shoulder ailment and always seems to miss part of each season. His absence proved very costly in 1983 when he went on the disabled list on August 1, disrupting our starting rotation as we pursued the Baltimore Orioles.

We got seven innings today before Milt faltered. His legs tired and he began to lose his control. Pitching coaches must spot this danger signal and bring it to the attention of the manager, who generally concerns himself with other facets of the game. This is a characteristic of Milt's. He's not a complete-game pitcher and does have a history of arm ailments. We can't expect nine innings from him if he's going to give us six months.

Willie showed me something, too. We brought him into the game at the outset of the eighth inning, and even though he allowed one run, he battled a case of the flu as well as the White Sox to earn his first save. "I have a sore throat, a head-ache, and a fever, but my arm feels good. I'll try to go out there and do my job," Hernandez told me. He even suffered from some dizziness, but his mere presence discouraged Chicago manager Tony LaRussa from going to his bench and calling on left-handed hitting Greg Walker, who hit three home runs against us last season.

The use of Willie was unusual considering his illness. Sparky and I had to make a decision, mindful that we would have received feedback from the press if Willie had been in-effective. We determined that his illness was not serious. If I keep a guy out of the lineup every time he has a hangnail or doesn't feel well, we won't have enough players to field a team.

I've never been second-guessed by the front office or Sparky. That's one reason we have such a fine relationship.

   I have to wonder how we fared as well as we did the previous four seasons without a quality left-handed reliever. We took a lot of flak when we acquired Willie this spring from the Phillies. Many members of the media criticized us for parting with two fan favorites. I can't deny the popularity of Wilson and Wockenfuss, but popularity contests don't win pennants.

   I spent some time on the bench discussing game situations with Glenn Abbott, a veteran pitcher we acquired last August from the Seattle Mariners. Abbott doesn't have the quality of pitches of Morris or Petry. He does know pitching theory, however, and we exchanged views on how to work a hitter with a runner on second base and first base open. In most instances, the hitter will be looking for breaking pitches or trick pitches because he realizes you have the luxury of walking him. We agreed that the best approach is to jam the hitter with fastballs. Most of the time the hitter will subsequently jam himself.

TIGERS 3, WHITE SOX 2   3 – 0

PITCHER	IP	H	R-ER	BB	SO	ERA
Wilcox (1-0)	7.0	4	1-1	4	2	1.29
Hernandez (S1)	2.0	2	1-1	0	1	1.80

J ACK Morris had no-hit stuff for the second game in a row. Too bad Gordon Lakey wasn't on hand to see it. Morris earned a spot in the Hall of Fame today by defeating the White Sox, 4-0, to become the first Tiger to pitch a no-hit game since Jim Bunning in 1958. The only mistake was the jubilant hug on the mound after Jack completed his gem by striking out Ron Kittle. The dugout, which collectively had held its breath, exploded in joy. Jack and catcher Lance Parrish tried to embrace. Instead, they looked like a pair of rams butting one

another. I decided it was good practice for the World Series.

No one can predict a no-hitter, but Jack definitely had the proper frame of mind entering the game. I asked him what kind of mood he was in and he nodded affirmatively with steely eyes intended for the White Sox. This is my way of measuring a pitcher's attitude immediately prior to his starting assignment. Quite often, that attitude isn't verbalized, but there usually is something revealing in his reaction. Jack was intense.

Luck is the lady on the arm of any no-hit pitcher and Jack enjoyed that company. I certainly don't mean to detract from his accomplishment, but there were three stages of the game where luck came into play. The first occurred in the first inning when leadoff hitter Rudy Law drove right fielder Kirk Gibson to the wall for his line drive. Gibson is an untested right fielder who is working extremely hard to become a good fielder. One adjustment he has made to capitalize on his speed and ability to charge balls is to play deeper than normal. This allowed Gibson to catch Law's drive.

The second stroke of luck occurred in the sixth inning. Catcher Carlton Fisk attempted to drop a bunt down the third base line. The bunt was perfectly placed, but spun foul. Jack still had that lady on his arm in the seventh inning when Tom Paciorek lined to first baseman Dave Bergman. Dave was playing off the bag because Greg Luzinski, a notoriously slow runner, was on first with a walk. Sparky admitted later that he would have had Bergman holding almost any other runner on first, which would have allowed Paciorek's line drive to reach right field for a base hit.

There was one point when not only the no-hitter but the outcome of the game was in jeopardy. Jack walked the first three batters in the fourth inning. He got out of it, though, when Luzinski tapped a split-fingered fastball back to him for a double play by way of home plate.

Baseball superstition insists that a no-hit bid never be interrupted by the mention of the possibility. We were obediently observing that superstition, but Jack didn't. There was a drunk seated behind our dugout, and beginning in the fifth inning he would lean over the top of the dugout and say, "You've got a no-hitter, Morris, you've got a no-hitter, Morris, and you're going to lose it." Finally, after the seventh inning, Jack said to the drunk, "I know I've got a no-hitter, and you just sit back and watch the next two innings because I'm going to get it." That shocked the superstitious types in our dugout, but also broke the tension.

Jack seemed to throw harder with a national television audience. National coverage would have affected a lot of pitchers, but Jack is such an outstanding competitor that he gained incentive from the camera's eye.

In my mind, Jack exemplified the attitude I try to arm every pitcher with before every game: Think perfect game, then think no-hitter, and then think shutout. Why not? I sat in the dugout of the Brooklyn Dodgers when Don Larsen, of the New York Yankees, pitched a perfect game in the 1956 World Series. Milt Wilcox came within one out of a perfect game in this same ballpark one year ago. Jack said at the time he could imagine the feelings Milt was experiencing must be unbelievable, and if he ever carried a no-hitter into the ninth inning he would get it.

Kittle had a good line, saying, "All in all, I'd rather have watched Morris bowl a perfect 300 game."

TIGERS 4, WHITE SOX 0   4 – 0

PITCHER	IP	H	R-ER	BB	SO	ERA
Morris (2-0)	9.0	0	0-0	6	8	0.56

Tigers who have pitched no-hitters:

George Mullin, 7-0 versus St. Louis on July 4, 1912
Virgil Trucks, 1-0 versus Washington on May 15, 1952
Virgil Trucks, 1-0 versus New York on August 25, 1952
Jim Bunning, 3-0 versus Boston on July 20, 1958
Jack Morris, 4-0 versus Chicago on April 7, 1984

THE day after was a blur for Morris. Jack said, "I think the part I liked best was sitting in the trainer's room after everyone had cleared out. Trammell, Brookens, Parrish, and Pio DiSalvo [head trainer] were my company. We were like a family rehashing what had happened. We got together later that night and shared a split of champagne. I just told the operator to hold all the calls to my room.

"I guess I still don't grasp the significance of my accomplishment. The morning papers said I had matched the record for throwing the earliest no-hitter. Whoopee! I mean, it's not as if I've never won a game before. Some day this will kick in, but right now I think what I want most is a little solitude.

"I know when we get home tonight the phone will be ringing. On Monday I have to be up early to appear on *Good Morning America.* To me, there's only one story that resulted from Saturday's game, and that was the fact we won. I've suffered through enough Septembers when guys are only playing hard in an attempt to make more money the next season.

"I usually go hunting in Utah or Montana every October. This year, I'd rather be pitching."

Jack is still in a dream world. He's underestimating his accomplishment. There's a tremendous amount of publicity that accompanies a no-hitter. I guess he didn't realize what he had done.

The furor created by Jack's no-hit game certainly didn't distract us today. We beat the White Sox, 7-3, thanks to four fine innings of relief from Aurelio Lopez. He and Hernandez provide us with what I call our Latin Connection. Dave Rozema started and I thought he would perform well after his outing on Monday in Minnesota, but he experienced the same stiffness that bothered him during spring training. We removed Rozie in the fifth inning when it became obvious from the bench that his arm was stiffening. Pitchers cannot disguise stiffness. They have a tendency to subject their pitching arm to extra movement between pitches and their delivery becomes unorthodox because they favor the arm. We're concerned about Dave's physical condition. He simply lacks strength and stamina, and that makes it tough to find a spot for him. He should be most effective as a six-inning starting pitcher. This would allow him proper rest between starts, but we might have to settle for spotting him in relief.

I will say this on Dave's behalf. When I went to the mound in the fifth inning he was very honest. He knew that if he survived that inning a victory was within his grasp, but he didn't fib. Dave thought he could get through the inning, while admitting his foremost concern was a victory for the team. A pitching coach appreciates that quality in a pitcher. I made the decision to bring in Lopez.

Lopez gave us four excellent innings, relying primarily on his fastball. Aurelio can pinpoint that fastball as well as any pitcher I've seen. A lot of pitchers know how to work hitters, but their lack of control prevents them from doing so.

TIGERS 7, WHITE SOX 3   5 – 0

PITCHER	IP	H	R-ER	BB	SO	ERA
Rozema	4 0	5	2-2	1	1	4.50
Lopez (1-0)	4.0	1	1-1	1	4	1.80
Hernandez	1.0	1	0-0	0	1	1.50

A 5-0 record can get a lot of people worked up. The city of Detroit and the state of Michigan is buzzing over "their" Tigers, and we don't mind one bit. Milt Wilcox says his friends tell him that people are walking through the malls with headphones on, listening to our games. Everything seems alive and fresh in this city, which has had its share of economic woes and hasn't been able to celebrate a baseball championship since the 1972 Tigers won the East Division. That's twelve years of frustration.

I always look for good omens. Today I decided the park was one. Tiger Stadium last season looked awful. Paint was peeling on the outside to the point that the stadium's exterior was offensive to me. What a difference this year! A little paint and a lot of siding has Tiger Stadium outfitted for national attention, which is just around the corner the way we're playing.

The last thing we want is to allow any negative thinking to infiltrate the clubhouse, so I called Sparky today at his condominium and emphasized the importance of positive thinking on the bench. I suggested that we have a meeting with the coaches to eliminate all negative thinking and negative remarks. That type of lapse can adversely affect a ballclub. Sparky agreed.

We have our home opener tomorrow, so I just kicked back in my apartment in West Bloomfield. Days like this one seem endless. Baseball offers a variety of advantages—travel, competition, and camaraderie leap to my mind, but there is nothing to replace the loneliness of an off-day at home without my wife, Carolyn. She's in Durham visiting her mother, and I'm in West Bloomfield missing her.

We've been married thirty-two years. I'll never forget the time I was making $88 a month and we were living in a dilapidated apartment. That we survived is hard to believe. That we survived so well is a blessing, manifested in our four children— Sherri, 31, Roger, Jr., 28, Teresa, 24, and Vikki, 22, and our three grandchildren, Michelle, 8, Melissa, 3, and Robin, 2. One

day soon I'm going to remind this lady how much I love her.
Right now, I'm going to think of the best way for Petry to beat
the Texas Rangers tomorrow.

There are several factors that coincide with a winning effort. Foremost, your starting pitcher must pitch to his strength.
Certainly the Rangers have players who are considered low
fastball hitters. This doesn't mean that Dan can desert his
fastball. We also rely on the opponent report submitted by
Boots Day. He alerts us to team tendencies: who steals and on
what count? What situation is most liable to produce a hit and
run? Who's hitting extremely well and what pitch is he hitting?
The game isn't any easier than the preparation, even though
some people are under the impression that pitching coaches
do nothing more than watch the day's starting pitcher warm
up in the bullpen.

One of my primary responsibilities in a game involves
signs—the silent conveyance of subsequent actions. I call 90
percent of the pitcher's tosses to first base when that base is
occupied by a runner. I also call all pitchouts. In addition, I steal
signs of the opposing club. I like to key on the manager. Quite
honestly, I wish the dugout in Detroit offered a better vantage
point. The dugouts in Tiger Stadium are so short in length that
the angle from the far corner of our dugout doesn't allow you
to peer into the near corner of the opposing dugout.

Signs can be conveyed to coaches and players in a variety
of ways. Some managers prefer hand signals. Others fold their
arms, and still others flash fingers. One finger, for example,
represents the take sign for the batter. Two could be the bunt,
three the hit and run, and four the steal. Slight head movements are the style of other managers. A movement to the
right could signify the hit and run, while movement to the left
the steal. A bowed head could mean a bunt is in order, while
a straight-ahead look is the take. Most managers will station
a coach alongside them to serve as a decoy. The coach will
be going through a whole series of meaningless movements,
usually hand signals. I carry a microcassette with me throughout the season to record all signs and opposing pitchers' moves
to first base from the stretch position.

Sparky likes to steal or hit and run frequently if the opposing pitcher has a high leg kick on his delivery from the stretch, or if the pitcher has an obvious pattern while holding runners on base. Some pitchers, for instance, will never throw to first if they come to a set position with their glove above the belt, but will if the glove is at or below the belt. I try to detect opposition pitchouts while we're at bat. There is a great advantage to stealing if you're certain the opposition won't pitch out. Once we determine that is the case we can use a flash sign from the bench to initiate a steal or hit and run. This is a fascinating game within the game that helps determine the final outcome.

Another function of mine is to track the use of players on lineup cards in the dugout. It is imperative to avoid overlooking players still available to your team or the opponent's team. The number of left-handed or right-handed hitters still at the disposal of the opposing managers will help shape your strategy in the late innings when you might have to go to your bullpen. You begin to think ahead and study possible matchups when the game is on the line. Does the opposition have a feared right-handed hitter if we bring in Willie Hernandez? Can the opposition counter with a left-handed reliever if Sparky summons John Grubb to pinch hit? I am constantly going over all possibilities with Sparky. He may not always agree, but he wants to be aware of his options rather than sit in the clubhouse after a loss and wonder why he refrained from making a specific move.

Many managers are too obstinate to seek the opinions of their coaches, but not Sparky. Our third base coach, Alex Grammas, who served on Sparky's staff for many years in Cincinnati, told me when I first arrived in Detroit in 1980 that it's impossible to be mad at Sparky. Alex is absolutely right. Sparky treats his coaches with a great deal of respect and puts more energy into his job than anyone I've known.

We played together in 1954 at Pueblo, Colorado, in the Brooklyn Dodgers organization. I'll always remember a game I pitched against Wichita. I had a no-hitter with two outs in the ninth inning, but walked the bases loaded one out from a victory and a possible shot at a pitcher's dream. Gordie Holt, our manager, strolled to the mound and hooked me. I was incredulous. Young George Anderson, our second baseman, was amused. That cockeyed smile he flashes creased his face.

I asked Sparky after the game if he felt Holt had made the correct move. "Rog," said Sparky, "he had to try to win the game and not think about your personal deeds. You had walked seven guys. You'd just walked the bases loaded. He did the right thing." The next year I was in the major leagues and the World Series, and Sparky was still in Class A posing as a player and preparing to be a manager.

Just as Sparky and I are compatible, so are our wives. Carol Anderson and Carolyn attend games together and stay out of the limelight. They are homebodies who prefer to shop at K-Mart rather than Saks Fifth Avenue. The four of us get together at Sparky's condominium every Sunday evening the club is at home. We usually sprinkle our conversation with family talk, but Sparky always returns to baseball.

He believes a manager should never lose a game and tries to accomplish this by winning around the clock. Sparky wants to be the best manager in the history of baseball and acts accordingly. I've never seen anyone who gets so high at one moment and so low the next, but he has great rapport with his players and is an expert at motivation. Sparky can detect the little things, such as personal problems, that could impede the internal progress of a team battling for the pennant. He'll discover that problem and weed it out before it becomes magnified.

Sparky and I began a practice in spring training that has carried over into the regular season: we take morning strolls whether we're at home or on the road. Ernie Harwell, the Tigers' Hall of Fame broadcaster, often accompanies us on these leisurely jaunts and his company is encouraged. If everyone grew up to be an Ernie Harwell, this world would be perfect. The walks provide good physical exercise and, more importantly, good mental therapy. Sparky and I discuss a wide range of subjects. We don't always agree, but I'm there to listen as he gets a lot of concerns off his chest.

BEFORE our home opener Sparky had a meeting of all the coaches to talk about positive thinking. All coaches have been guilty at one time or another of sitting on the bench and suddenly without thinking saying "This guy isn't a good major league player" or "This guy can't run." The players don't want to hear this. I felt this was the proper time to make sure this practice was eliminated. If the coaches want to discuss negatives, it must be done in private. The meeting was lengthy but the response from all the coaches was good.

Dan Petry gave our Opening Day crowd of more than 50,000 a good reason to celebrate by going the distance to defeat the Texas Rangers 5-1. Dan used all four of his pitches. I asked Sparky to let Dan finish the game because that would boost his confidence. The four-hit performance was remarkable given the electricity of Opening Day. The home opener always is hectic. Players arrive early because they are filled with anticipation—and want to make sure their new home uniforms fit properly.

Tom Monaghan, who purchased the Tigers from John E. Fetzer last October for the tidy sum of $50 million, arrived in his helicopter. Monaghan spent some time in the clubhouse in Lakeland, Florida, during spring training, but did not enter our clubhouse today. That was tactful. No one wants an owner who meddles. I feel Monaghan has decided to leave the baseball operation to baseball people, such as club president Jim Campbell. I hope I'm correct.

Home openers offer a sudden awareness that the season has begun, a rebirth of a life that ended only months earlier. Petry blocked all this out and conquered his own excitement to run our record to 6-0.

Dan is twenty-five years old. The victory today was the sixty-first of his promising career. I made my major league debut at the age of twenty-four with the 1955 Brooklyn Dodgers and retired in 1966 with seventy-four major league victories.

Michigan Gov. James Blanchard at our home opener

I was proud of every one of them and some of the losses, too. I see the same qualities in Petry. He signed a four-year contract worth $3.6 million this past winter. Dan envies Al Kaline because Kaline spent his entire major league career in a Tiger uniform. He realizes that the confrontation between pitcher and batter is the ultimate distillation of the game. He grew up admiring the sheer simplicity and enormous domination of Nolan Ryan's fastball. Dan wants victories and he'll certainly earn his share.

After the game the clubhouse was crowded with reporters and Sparky said something I greatly appreciate. He told the reporters he could take a prolonged vacation in Bermuda and the Tigers would never miss him, but that the Tigers would be in a fine mess if they lost Roger Craig.

Before the game a photographer was circulating 11 × 14 pictures of Jack Morris and Lance Parrish botching their hug following Jack's no-hit game in Chicago. I asked Jack to inscribe a personal message on the photo I purchased, and this time he was perfect.

"To Roger,
"One minute of joy for hours of hard work.
You've been an inspiration to me
and I'm proud to have you as my pitching coach
and friend."

Sparky, Billy Consolo, and I went to a party at the Roostertail restaurant after the game. The attitude of the fans in this town is amazing. I believe this is the most enthusiastic baseball town I've been in. Detroit reminds me a lot of Brooklyn.

Everyone is behind us, including the other six teams in the East Division.

TIGERS 5, RANGERS 1   6 – 0

PITCHER	IP	H	R-ER	BB	SO	ERA
Petry (2-0)	9.0	4	1-1	3	7	1.69

The league's best one-two pitching punch — Petry and Morris

I got a Texas-sized boot out of a comment made by Larry Parrish of the Rangers. He said that Jack Morris and Dan Petry are the toughest pitchers in the league to face back-to-back and that the Tigers are going to lose sometime this season. Parrish really made me chuckle when he added, "It's tough to throw two no-hitters in a row." We would gladly settle for our seventh consecutive victory. The Tigers have been in this business since 1900 without ever winning their first seven games. I'll say right now that our ambitions transcend a 7-0 start.

JOHNNY Vander Meer, the only major league pitcher ever to hurl back-to-back no-hit games, can sleep peacefully tonight. Jack Morris didn't get another no-hitter, but he did notch another victory, as we defeated the Texas Rangers 9-4. Mickey Rivers dispensed with the no-hit suspense in a hurry by lining Jack's fifth pitch of the game to left field for a single.

Jack's fastball wasn't popping and he didn't have a very good split-fingered fastball. I reminded him during the game that to be effective without exceptional action on his pitches would depend on pitch selection, intense concentration, and pitch location. A pitcher with good stuff, or darting pitches, can survive mistakes because of the movement of the ball. When the action of the ball is substandard, the pitcher must rely on other weapons. I encouraged Jack to concentrate on the glove of Lance Parrish as his target, and he prevailed with the support of home runs by Chet Lemon, Alan Trammell, and Lou Whitaker.

This game put us in the Tigers' record book. I could feel the surge of optimism.

Sparky and I decided to remove Jack after seven innings. We enjoyed another large cushion (9-2) and we want to avoid burnout. Aurelio Lopez and Willie Hernandez pitched one inning apiece. Aurelio permitted two runs, which served as no surprise. He's a very emotional person who is most effective in save or win situations with the game hanging in the balance. Aurelio tends to lose concentration in lopsided games, a lapse that usually results in runs. Willie didn't throw as well as normal, as he allowed one hit and one walk. His inning served a purpose, though. He relishes heavy duty and we want to be certain he receives enough work so that he's operating at peak efficiency when games become more snug.

I am mildly concerned about the physical condition of Lopez. He has experienced some swelling on the back of his pitching hand. Aurelio had the same problem last season and we suffered because he saved only two games for us the final two months after chalking up sixteen saves through July. Dr. Clarence Livingood, our team physician, drained 2 cc. of fluid from Aurelio's injured pitching hand following the game. Livingood determined that Aurelio is suffering from gout, and placed him on medication and a more nutritional diet. Livingood also recommended that Lopez not consume any alcohol. Sparky and I intend to make sure Lopez adheres to Livingood's wishes.

We have too good a ballclub to risk losing a championship because of one person's eating habits.

TIGERS 9, RANGERS 4   7 – 0

PITCHER	IP	H	R-ER	BB	SO	ERA
Morris (3-0)	7.0	7	2-0	1	2	0.39
Lopez	1.0	2	2-2	1	0	4.50
Hernandez	1.0	1	0-0	1	0	1.29

WILCOX blew a chance for a cinch victory today. We gave him an eight-run working margin in the first inning, and he returned five of those runs to prematurely force us into our bullpen. Milt threw only twenty-four pitches, all of which were forgettable. Doug Bair came in and saved us with four and one-third innings of one-run relief. Bair struck out five batters in helping to ruin the Boston Red Sox home opener, 13-9. Afterwards he was barbing Petry about career strikeouts. Bair has 474, Dan has 472. With all due respect to Doug, I'll bet a fancy western belt buckle that Dan winds up on top. Glenn Abbott also pitched and gave us two scoreless innings to preserve a three-run lead. Glenn escaped a bases-loaded predicament in the sixth inning when he deflected a hard ground ball hit by Rick Miller off his left heel to shortstop Alan Trammell for an inning-ending double play. That ball should have been a two-run single.

Pitching with an eight-run lead is not the easiest assignment, especially in Fenway Park and in Boston's home opener. Boston fans have the same enthusiasm for baseball as Tiger followers and Fenway has the same nostalgic charm as Tiger Stadium. Fenway also has the Green Monster—the imposing left-field wall that invites home runs and poses a psychological problem for pitchers. I urge my pitchers to ignore it, which is difficult when facing a lineup that includes legitimate home run hitters such as Jim Rice, Tony Armas, and Dwight Evans. The main objective is to keep from altering your pattern of pitching.

Milt wasn't affected as much by the configuration of Fenway Park as he was by negative thoughts. Pitchers sometimes have a tendency to expect negative results. They too closely chart what might happen if they walk a batter with a three-run lead and the potential tying run eventually comes to bat. This is asking for trouble, and trouble frequently accepts that invitation. Positive thinking is essential at all times, and Milt did not prove to be a disciple of Norman Vincent Peale. Milt was look-ing for bad things to happen and they did.

Lance Parrish received all the media attention after the game. Lance wears No. 13 and this was Friday the thirteenth.

Lance, the man behind the mask, has no equal

COURTESY THE DETROIT TIGERS

Parrish accounted for all our outs in the first inning by striking out with the bases loaded and grounding into a double play with the bases loaded as the thirteenth batter in our half of an inning that produced thirteen runs. Lance did make amends with a home run and scored our thirteenth run of the game in a four-run eighth inning.

Lance is a fine human being, the kind of person you'd like a son to be. He was very reserved in his early years. He now knows the pitching pattern of each pitcher on the staff. Lance understands how best to set up hitters for each pitcher. He has improved at making adjustments during the course of a game. If Milt Wilcox, for instance, isn't getting his split-fingered fastball over, Lance reverts to the curve or fastball for a while, possibly to return to the split-fingered fastball later. Lance visits the mound more frequently now, which I like. I can't be running out to the mound all the time. Lance has learned to sense when a pitcher is running a little scared. He'll just go to the mound and remind the pitcher to go with his best pitches, and not to squeeze or guide the ball. I have an intricate series of signs and must have a bright catcher, which Lance is. He also has obvious physical talents which benefit the pitching staff. His arm is as strong as any catcher's in baseball and this affects an opposing manager's game plan. He is a real deterrent to base stealing.

One afterthought on this game: we turned six double plays, which tied a major league record. A pitcher can't ask for much more than thirteen runs and six double plays.

TIGERS 13, RED SOX 9   8 – 0

PITCHER	IP	H	R-ER	BB	SO	ERA
Wilcox	0.2	4	5-5	1	0	7.04
Bair (1-0)	4.1	3	1-1	1	5	2.08
Abbott	2.0	2	0-0	1	0	0.00
Hernandez	2.0	5	3-3	2	2	4.00

W E'RE savoring our 8-0 rush on an off-day and I'm thinking about the split-fingered fastball, which I believe has been vital to our success. I've researched this pitch extensively and even tried to throw it during my career, but without the same success enjoyed by most of my pitchers. I've talked a lot with Bruce Sutter, of the St. Louis Cardinals, and I watched Lindy McDaniel and Elroy Face throw the split-finger during their playing days. That prompted me to introduce the pitch to teenagers at a baseball school I used to own in San Diego before selling my share to Alan Trammell. The split-finger is a good off-speed pitch that can be thrown at virtually every level of play. Junior high school or even little league isn't too early because this pitch doesn't put strain on the arm and requires only an average-sized hand. Gaylord Perry wasn't too old to pick up the split-finger at the age of forty as a complement to his spitter.

The key to an effective split-finger is to think fastball. Common sense tells you if you throw a fastball with your fingers split apart you won't deliver that pitch with the same velocity as a fastball. Hold the ball with the seams, much like a sinking fastball, and deliver the pitch with a natural fastball motion. This gives the pitch its deception. Begin by spreading the fingers about one-half inch apart and gradually keep spreading them while working the ball down toward your palm. Some guys, like Jack Morris, can get the ball deep in their hand and some, like Milt Wilcox, keep the ball out toward their fingertips. Don't grip the ball too deeply. The important thing is to assume a grip which feels comfortable and allows you to throw strikes. You can concentrate on the thumb once you feel comfortable gripping the ball with your middle and index fingers. Try to manipulate the thumb by imparting a little pressure upon release of the ball. This will give the pitch a tumbling effect. You also can curl the fingertips of your middle and index fingers, especially the index finger. That friction will give the pitch even more of a tumbling effect. Guard against choking the ball. Choking means setting the ball too deep in your hand. This results in a false sense that you have to throw harder than normal. Get the ball as far out on your fingertips as possible, and try to have a slight gap between the ball and your middle and index fingers. Also, try to exert a little pressure on the ball with the top joints of your middle and index fingers at the point of release. This, too, will give the ball a greater tumbling effect.

Morris, Wilcox, Petry, Rozema, Abbott, and Berenguer use the split-fingered fastball. I'm attempting to convince Doug Bair to throw it because I feel it's a natural for him. I do believe I'll prevail.

WE won our ninth straight, 4-3, in ten innings over the Kansas City Royals. This puts us within two games of matching the 1981 Oakland A's for the best start in American League history. I don't really endorse these so-called records. Maybe that's why our eighth victory slipped my mind, even though it did represent the best start by any Tiger team. Morris failed to record his fourth consecutive victory. Jack had a 3-0 lead in the eighth inning. Then he surrendered a three-run home run to Jorge Orta after Pat Sheridan had fouled off a lot of good pitches and hit a split-fingered fastball to right field for a single.

Orta's home run came on a low fastball over the middle of the plate, a definite mistake pitch on Jack's part. Orta dines on low fastballs. He has to be pitched fastballs up and in or breaking pitches.

Jack's mistake cost him the lead and a personal victory. He was hampered by a below-average split-fingered fastball. Jack was choking the ball too much and that restricts the tumbling effect. Full command of his split-fingered fastball will result in eight to ten strikeouts per game. Jack had only three strikeouts today.

Willie Hernandez pitched the tenth inning and gained credit for his first American League victory when second baseman Frank White bobbled a ground ball hit by Larry Herndon to allow the winning run to score. Willie shows signs of being an outstanding relief pitcher. He's really establishing his fastball inside and this makes his screwball, which runs away from right-handed hitters, a potent weapon.

After four consecutive days of inactivity because of three rainouts and one scheduled off-day, we needed a good dose of pre-game work down in the bullpen. I changed the grip on Berenguer's breaking ball so its movement is not so sweeping. I also detected a mechanical flaw in Abbott's delivery. He was throwing across his body and blocking himself off, which is a

A little advice is helpful at a time like this

major problem for a control pitcher such as Glenn. Milt Wilcox has been choking his split-fingered fastball too much. We relaxed the grip and the pitch was dipping like an express elevator headed for the lobby. Milt will pitch on Friday against the Chicago White Sox and I'm anxious to see how he fares.

Right now I'm just relieved to have another victory to our credit.

TIGERS 4, ROYALS 3 *(10 innings)* 9 — 0

PITCHER	IP	H	R-ER	BB	SO	ERA
Morris	9.0	9	3-3	0	3	1.13
Hernandez (1-0)	1.0	0	0-0	0	1	3.60

W E built a nine-game winning streak by defeating established pitchers such as Richard Dotson, Floyd Bannister,
Tom Seaver, and Frank Tanana. The streak ended today when
we were humbled by a twenty-year-old youngster who has
spent more time as the shortstop for the Universal Studios
softball team than as a professional pitcher.

I have to tip my cap to Bret Saberhagen. He checked us
on one run through six innings to help the Kansas City Royals
hand us our first defeat, 5-2. I've seen better stuff from young
pitchers, but never as much poise as Saberhagen took to the
mound for his first major league start. He must have felt he
was picking grounders back at Universal Studios where he
worked two and one-half years on the clean-up crew. Our advance description of Saberhagen was a cross between Mel
Stottlemyre and Catfish Hunter. For one day, that description
was accurate.

Petry gave us a good effort in defeat. He was hurt by a
pair of errors by third baseman Howard Johnson and was
tagged in the eighth inning for a two-run home run by Frank
White following a two-out walk to Steve Balboni. The walk
stemmed from tentative pitching. Dan was intent on keeping
us within one run of the Royals. The eighth inning is a critical
period for any starting pitcher who is beginning to tire and is
vulnerable to making mistakes. Dan's biggest mistake was the
walk; his second biggest was the home run pitch to White.

Johnson's errors, which contributed to an unearned run
in the sixth inning, were not welcomed, but are an accepted
part of the game. Players who commit errors need reassurance
from the pitcher, who must harbor no grudges. An encouraging word lifts the fielder's spirits and makes the pitcher a
better man. Pitchers must voice this encouragement immediately and must never under any circumstances show up a
teammate. Errors are not made intentionally. In this case, Dan
told Howard, "Don't worry about it. Sometime you'll hit a home

run to win a game like this." Lopez worked the ninth inning and gave us every indication that he has conquered his bout with gout.

Saberhagen is worth a couple of footnotes to illustrate the manner in which an intelligent pitcher can work hitters. He struck out Darrell Evans on a full-count sinker in the first inning with runners on first and third and no outs. That marked the first time Saberhagen had shown Evans that particular pitch, and it showed me a lot of confidence and courage in a sticky situation. Saberhagen also struck out Johnson on a full-count changeup with Chet Lemon on third base and one out in the fifth inning. Lemon represented the tying run. The changeup was the first Johnson had seen from Saberhagen in two at-bats. Give the kid credit.

ROYALS 5, TIGERS 2   9 – 1

PITCHER	IP	H	R-ER	BB	SO	ERA
Petry (2-1)	8.0	8	5-4	2	4	3.04
Lopez	1.0	0	0-0	0	0	3.86

Good pitching and fielding by Milt Wilcox beat the White Sox

FRIDAY, APRIL 20   DETROIT

THE news accounts of tonight's game will report we won on a disputed call in the ninth inning. I contend we won in the sixth inning thanks to an outstanding play by Milt Wilcox. Any pitcher can enhance his status by capably fielding his position. Wilcox did that when he pounced on a Scott Fletcher bunt. He fired the ball to Tom Brookens, retiring Rudy Law on a tag play at third base. We trailed 2-1 at the time and Milt's play not only prevented the Chicago White Sox from mounting a two-run lead, but also provided us with some momentum. We tied the game in the seventh inning and won in the ninth when Ron Kittle's catch of a looping fly ball by Lance Parrish was ruled a trap. Lance's ball seemed like a hang glider frozen forever in mid-air. When it finally came down we claimed a 3-2 victory to raise our record to 10-1. I thought Kittle caught the ball. We received the benefit of the doubt on a tough call. One team always does.

Milt pitched well except for a two-run home run by Kittle on a split-fingered fastball. This is the pitch we've been working

on. Apparently, it needs more work. Milt was the first pitcher on our staff to convert to the split-finger. In 1981, I convinced him to junk his slider, which was leaving the park too frequently. I'm considering an alternate plan for Milt, which is to use his curveball more often. He throws his curve at two speeds—a typically hard curve and one that squirts out of his hand as an off-speed delivery. That would serve the same purpose as the split-fingered fastball. This is an example of the adjustments which have to be made during the course of any season.

Aurelio Lopez deservedly received credit for the victory. He pitched the ninth inning and gave us further reason to believe he is on the road to a complete recovery. Aurelio had complete command of his fastball, especially up and in to hitters.

I worked before the game with Morris and with Berenguer, who will make his first appearance of the season on Sunday. Juan is throwing a new slider, which isn't real good yet. I think he will benefit from the pitch, though, because he can throw it for strikes.

Jack concentrated on his split-fingered fastball. He's choking the pitch to death. We moved his fingers out and more on top of the ball, instead of spread wide apart. This should improve his command of the pitch. Jack doesn't have to throw the split-fingered fastball in the strike zone. The pitch must only appear to be a strike before dropping from the strike zone in the final instant—after the batter has committed himself.

Dave Rozema will start tomorrow. I'm looking forward to that. Dave's throwing a small slider which I feel will improve his effectiveness. We're hoping for five or six good innings. We tell all our starting pitchers to strive for nine innings, but in Dave's case, seven would be frosting on the cake. We must anticipate going to the bullpen whenever Dave starts.

TIGERS 3, WHITE SOX 2   10 − 1

PITCHER	IP	H	R-ER	BB	SO	ERA
Wilcox	8.0	8	2-2	3	3	4.59
Lopez (2-0)	1.0	0	0-0	0	1	3.38

DAVE Rozema against LaMarr Hoyt may not seem a very favorable matchup, but neither was David and Goliath! Rozema limited the Chicago White Sox to two hits over six innings. We decked Hoyt 4-1 to sever his fifteen-game winning streak, which was only two shy of matching the major league record.

Rozema has been a man-child for us over the years. He's a bit of a rounder who loves to indulge in innocent pranks which invariably become catastrophes. There have been plenty of times when we considered trading Dave. This past winter, in fact, his name was discussed, but I encouraged Sparky and general manager Bill Lajoie to exercise caution. You can tolerate certain shortcomings if a player has talent. Dave knows how to pitch. He's not blessed with the greatest stuff, but he knows how to set up hitters and change speeds. He also locates his pitches as well as any pitcher I've coached. Dave seems to have matured, probably because he's faced with the stark reality that this is the final year of a three-year contract. He's only twenty-seven years old and isn't ready for life without baseball.

Dave admitted this spring to Dr. Clarence Livingood, our team physician, Sparky, and me that he felt he was drinking in excess. There were thoughts of professional help, but Dave believed he could discipline himself. Sparky and I had a long and frank discussion with him. He has cut back markedly on his consumption of alcohol, which has driven many undisciplined players from baseball.

Dave struck out seven White Sox, five of those called, by mixing a good sinker with sidearm curveballs. He even threw an uncalled-for pitch by freezing left-handed hitting Harold Baines with a sidearm curve. Baseball dictum says right-handed pitchers don't throw sidearm curves to left-handed hitters because the plane of the pitch is too flat. Tell that to Baines.

Doug Bair finished up and allowed one run. We left him in the game because he was throwing exceptionally hard into

One guy who's matured in the past year is Dave Rozema

the shadows covering home plate on a very cold day. Hitters don't exactly pop their buttons under such conditions.

One feature of our team that shouldn't go unnoticed is the improved play of Kirk Gibson in right field. Kirk made a good running catch in the right field corner today. He works exceedingly hard prior to every game. One of my pre-game duties is to hit fungoes to Kirk. His range and the way he goes back for fly balls have improved immensely. As pitching coach I don't mind the time spent hitting fungoes to an outfielder. Pitching is only as good as defense. Kirk will get to a lot of balls other outfielders won't reach. His play, along with that of the rest of our defense, will be reflected in the pitching statistics.

TIGERS 4, WHITE SOX 1   11 — 1

PITCHER	IP	H	R-ER	BB	SO	ERA
Rozema (1-0)	6.0	2	0-0	2	7	1.80
Bair (S1)	3.0	3	1-1	0	3	2.46

O N Easter Sunday Juan Berenguer overcame sleet and rain to earn us our sixth consecutive victory over the Chicago White Sox, 9-1.

This was Juan's first appearance of the season. He was demoralized when we removed him from the starting rotation. Juan was hurt and I had a big task to perform. I can keep a pitcher physically prepared to pitch, but leading him through mental gymnastics is more complex. Juan had to be mentally fit to pitch and he came out firing with a very powerful performance.

For three weeks we worked every other day in the bullpen. I focused on convincing Juan to be aggressive and to take charge. I told him to prove to us that taking him out of the rotation was a mistake. He did.

Juan allowed two hits and no runs in seven innings. I had to do a lot of fast talking to Sparky during a rain delay in the fifth inning to keep him in the game. Juan had a no-hitter at the time, but Sparky, who constantly needs to be impressed by Berenguer because Juan is not a polished pitcher, asked if I thought Juan should be lifted. I told him in no uncertain terms that Juan had to be allowed to continue because it just wouldn't be right to deprive him of a chance for a victory. Juan demonstrated patience and strong mental discipline waiting for this moment. Rain was not going to destroy three weeks of work.

White Sox manager Tony LaRussa left Detroit impressed with our club. He offered the opinion that we have a great chance to win our division. A team that frequently has Chet Lemon and Kirk Gibson batting in the lower third of the batting order carries some big sticks, he said. That assessment is correct, but don't overlook our pitching. This was the first series of the season in which neither Jack Morris nor Dan Petry were scheduled to pitch. I would be fibbing if I didn't admit we entered this series with some reservations about the strength of our second-line pitching. Those reservations have been erased. Milt, Dave, and Juan allowed two runs in twenty-one innings against the club that led the league in runs scored last season. This is ample reason for my swelling pride, especially since LaRussa was forced to summon first baseman Mike Squires to pitch to one batter in the eighth inning.

Our rookie catcher, Dwight Lowry, made his first major league start today and handled Juan perfectly. Dwight threw out one baserunner and called most of the pitches, although I did call a few. This is a practice we initiated in 1981 because we believed Lance Parrish needed a little guidance. Lance didn't like this practice. There's no question it was awkward. Every catcher likes to believe he can handle his staff, and every catcher assumes the pulse of a game can best be measured from behind the plate, not from the dugout. But there's nothing wrong with using the voice of experience on certain occasions. I believe Lance would agree now that this brief practice helped him grow as a major league catcher.

You must have a high level of communication between your pitchers and catchers. Naturally, the more a catcher works with a pitcher, the better the catcher will understand his pattern of pitching. There will be disagreements over which pitch to throw in certain situations. Pitchers sometimes shake off the pitch selection of their catcher, something catchers frown on as an affront to their intelligence. This is the time for communication and a trip to the mound by the catcher, who must explain why he feels his pitch selection is best. Maybe the hitter has moved up in the batter's box or made some other slight adjustment the pitcher has not noticed. Maybe the scouting report indicated the hitter has been having difficulty hitting that pitch. A persuasive catcher might instill confidence in the pitcher to throw a suggested pitch, but a pitcher must never throw a pitch that he doesn't have complete confidence in.

TIGERS 9, WHITE SOX 1   12 − 1

PITCHER	IP	H	R-ER	BB	SO	ERA
Berenguer (1-0)	7.0	2	0-0	1	7	0.00
Lopez	1.0	1	0-0	0	1	3.00
Hernandez	1.0	2	1-1	1	2	4.09

I guess our spate of victories ruffled the feathers of the World Champion Baltimore Orioles. They seized upon an isolated and innocent comment by Sparky Anderson in an attempt to derail our fast start. In a newspaper interview last week, Sparky said we would have fun in October. Ken Singleton, a player of high professional standards, countered that we're running the pennant flag up the pole a bit prematurely. Singleton said the Orioles don't have any games scheduled in October and observed that we don't either. Sparky's statement was simply a testament to the confidence he has in our team. The statement would have been ignored by the Orioles if they weren't off to a 2-10 start while we are 12-1.

Sparky always has had a loose and lively tongue. He is an impulsive man and, believe me, the coaching staff worked hard over the years to temper much of his impulsiveness. Sparky has some of the con in him. That is a common trait of virtually all managers who must sell their product rather than allowing the product to sell itself. Sparky's early Tiger teams *had* to be sold.

The Orioles are taking umbrage at any attempt on our part to peddle this year's club as a legitimate contender. They don't understand why Sparky is making media darlings out of players such as Alan Trammell, Lou Whitaker, Chet Lemon, and Lance Parrish. I believe they're afraid Sparky is correct.

TUESDAY, APRIL 24   DETROIT

D ETROIT is becoming the baseball capital of the country. An army of reporters has invaded our sanctuary. *Sports Illustrated* is here to do a feature on my pitching staff. Each day a strange face from out of town arrives to dissect our start. Local radio stations are playing songs that try to capture the atmosphere we've created in this town. As pitching coach, I am asked a broad range of questions about my pitching theories, the split-fingered fastball, and the development of my pitchers. Everyone seems intent on writing the definitive life story of Jack Morris.

The news media are very powerful. A pen really *can* be mightier than a sword. Anyone in the public eye should be aware of this. Reporters are no different than any other group of professionals—some are good, some are bad, some are mediocre. I try to oblige all of them. It's my job. You can't ignore the press, just as you can't hide from adversity. You must cope with reporters the same as with opposing hitters. Honesty generally is the best policy, although little white lies are sometimes required. The clubhouse is our season-long home, after all, and the club is a family of brothers.

We do not have written rules prohibiting players from participating in media hypes, but we certainly discourage anything that might distract from our principal goal of winning games. Kevin Saucier, Enos Cabell, and Larry Herndon recorded a song called "Ain't No Stopping Us Now" early in 1982, and we immediately lapsed into a prolonged slump. The record, needless to say, was never released.

We defeated the Minnesota Twins twice, 6-5 and 4-3, after trailing in both games. We captured the opener primarily because of mental mistakes by the Twins. Those strange twists resulted in a three-run ninth inning. Lance Parrish helped win the second game with a three-run home run that rubbed out a 3-1 deficit. Our record is 14-1.

Jack Morris did not have good command in the first game. He managed just one strikeout in nine innings. Kent Hrbek hit a fourth-inning home run off a two-strike fastball. This unnerved Jack a bit. Mental discipline is an area in which we've worked extremely hard with Jack. I will say that he normally would have blown his cool and lost the game. But this time he held on and shut out the Twins over the final four innings.

We removed Petry in the fourth inning of the second game because he's had a little tenderness in his pitching elbow. The injury was diagnosed as a strained tricep. It shouldn't stop him from taking his next turn here on Sunday against Cleveland.

Glenn Abbott replaced Dan and did allow two runs. Aurelio Lopez saved the game with three innings of shutout relief. Lopey's fastball is really popping, and he showed me an improved screwball after consulting with Willie Hernandez about the mechanics of that pitch. I worked with Juan Berenguer before the doubleheader. His cut fastball, a pitch that rides away slightly to right-handed batters and into left-handed batters, and his slider are improving rapidly.

These weren't pretty victories, but the fact we came from behind is a sign of champions. We've now been dubbed "Raiders of the Lost Game" by some members of the media.

After the games, we took a charter flight out of Windsor, Ontario, to Arlington, Texas, and were delayed by customs officials. They asked for identification! I had mine but Sparky had to debark to clear customs because he had left his valuables in the clubhouse. Jack stayed in Detroit because he isn't scheduled to pitch on this two-game, one-city trip.

TIGERS 6, TWINS 5 *(First game)*   13 − 1

PITCHER	IP	H	R-ER	BB	SO	ERA
Morris (4-0)	9.0	7	5-5	5	1	1.98

TIGERS 4, TWINS 3 *(Second game)*   14 − 1

PITCHER	IP	H	R-ER	BB	SO	ERA
Petry	3.0	2	1-1	2	1	3.00
Abbott (1-0)	3.0	3	2-2	1	2	3.60
Lopez (S1)	3.0	1	0-0	2	3	2.25

WEDNESDAY, APRIL 25   ARLINGTON

W E discuss pitching patterns with our pitchers and catchers prior to every series. We want to know precisely how we'll work opposing hitters in every conceivable situation. We also discuss theory, such as pitching backward. Pitching is essentially a sequential process that requires thinking like a hitter. Pitching backward is an inversion of the hitter's thinking—breaking balls when behind in the count rather than fastballs, and fastballs when ahead in the count. You don't get too scientific, however, if you possess an exceptional fastball. Glenn Abbott coined a new expression during the planning meeting in Texas before we lassoed the Texas Rangers 9-4. In a ribald description of an overpowering pitch that freezes the hitter, Glenn said he wants to throw a "Bowel Locker." Glenn now has a new nickname.

Milt Wilcox departed after six innings with a comfortable cushion and some stiffness in his pitching shoulder, perhaps attributable to a twenty-five mile per hour prairie wind that buffeted Arlington Stadium.

I check a pitcher's physical condition after every inning. You can't take anything for granted. I simply ask a pitcher how he feels and then make a judgment based as much on the inflection of his voice as on what he actually says. Milt wasn't totally positive in his response, so Willie Hernandez received some necessary work. Willie did not pitch well. His lead (left) shoulder is flying open on his cut fastball and he's not turning over his screwball. I'm convinced he merely needs more work.

TIGERS 9, RANGERS 4   15 – 1

PITCHER	IP	H	R-ER	BB	SO	ERA
Wilcox (2-0)	6.0	6	2-2	2	2	4.15
Hernandez (S2)	3.0	5	2-2	1	3	4.50

I feel sorry for Dick Such, the pitching coach of the Texas Rangers. Balls are flying out of Arlington Stadium like helium-filled balloons because of a jet stream to center field.

We beat the Rangers 7-5 to bump our record to 16-1 and are now within one win of matching the 1981 Oakland A's for the best eighteen-game start in league history.

Dave Rozema experienced stiffness in his neck and shoulder again, but I encouraged Sparky to let him pitch five innings and get credit for the victory. Sparky wanted to remove Dave with a 6-2 lead, two runners on base, and one out in the fifth inning. I disagreed. Sparky relented. Then Pete O'Brien hit a three-run home run off Dave. We didn't lose, but I accept the blame for leaving Dave in the game long enough for O'Brien to challenge our lead. I talked to Dave after the game and he was understandably upset. This had been a great opportunity for him to reward my confidence in him as a pitcher.

Doug Bair and Aurelio Lopez spared me some embarrassment by checking Texas over the final four innings. Bair has been an unsung hero as a middle reliever. He never complains. He just does his job, which usually offers no statistical reward. Lopez continues to look better each time he pitches. Lopey recorded his second save in as many games and has not permitted a run in his past eight and two-thirds innings. Dan Petry threw for ten minutes before the game and seems sufficiently recovered from his strained tricep to make his scheduled start on Sunday in Detroit against the Cleveland Indians.

The wind was brisk again tonight and drained us. We returned to Detroit following the game. When I nestled into bed it was exactly 5 A.M. Friday. When you're winning, though, you're not tired.

Doug Bair—the unsung hero of my staff

TIGERS 7, RANGERS 5   16 – 1

PITCHER	IP	H	R-ER	BB	SO	ERA
Rozema	4.1	7	5-5	0	1	4.40
Bair (2-0)	2.0	4	0-0	1	1	1.93
Lopez (S2)	2.2	0	0-0	0	2	1.84

FRIDAY, APRIL 27   DETROIT

W E didn't get much shuteye or a spot in the record book with the Oakland A's, but we did prove to be pretty good sleepwalkers. The Cleveland Indians beat us 8-4 in a nineteen-inning marathon that lasted nearly six hours. We are grateful that Jack Morris, tomorrow's starting pitcher, didn't make that taxing trip to Texas. We are also pleased that we had enough common sense to send him home tonight after the tenth inning. Jack was asleep before the game ended.

You would expect runs to be scattered all over the scoreboard in a nineteen-inning game, but only two were scored from the third inning through the eighteenth.

Juan Berenguer started for us and performed well, although he contributed to an unearned run by throwing the wrong pitch in a pitchout situation. That cost him a run and possibly the game. I use signs from the dugout to signal a pitchout. The pitcher and catcher must be able to interpret this body language correctly. Juan made a mistake. Instead of throwing a fastball high and outside to provide catcher Lance Parrish with the best possible opportunity to throw out base-stealer Brett Butler at second base, Berenguer threw a low split-fingered fastball over the plate. Parrish had vacated that area and Butler subsequently scored on a double by Julio Franco.

We lost on four unearned runs when Glenn Abbott misplayed two bunts into errors sometime around 1 A.M. on Saturday. The next day I told Glenn we were going to work on his fielding rather than his pitching, but I did it with a smile. Glenn was guilty of physical errors and he knew that. A baseball season lasts a long time and there's no reason to dwell on negative situations that can't be changed.

INDIANS 8, TIGERS 4 *(19 innings)*   16 – 2

PITCHER	IP	H	R-ER	BB	SO	ERA
Berenguer	7.2	8	3-1	3	6	0.61
Hernandez	1.2	1	1-1	1	2	4.60
Lopez	4.2	1	0-0	4	2	1.40
Abbott (1-1)	5.0	2	4-0	2	2	1.80

SATURDAY, APRIL 28   DETROIT

JACK Morris is the cure for a bullpen that worked eleven and one-third innings the previous night. What Jack missed in Texas and here last night hurt neither him nor the Tigers in the won-lost column. He rejoined us today and limited the Cleveland Indians to three singles in a 6-2 complete-game victory. But even though we can trace our success to the fact that he was fresh, many of his teammates were rankled that Jack did not make the trip to Texas.

That decision was not Jack's. Sparky and I felt that leaving Jack in Detroit would be in the club's best interest. The majority of players felt that Jack, as a member of the team, should have been in Texas in the dugout providing encouragement. Score one for the players.

We were in a sticky situation and Jack gave us nine very good innings. He now has pitched a minimum of seven innings in thirty-one of his past thirty-two starting assignments spanning two seasons.

TIGERS 6, INDIANS 2   17 – 2

PITCHER	IP	H	R-ER	BB	SO	ERA
Morris (5-0)	9.0	3	2-2	3	5	1.98

Jack Morris is just what the doctor ordered

SUNDAY, APRIL 29   DETROIT

THE Cleveland Indians were Petry-fied today, 6-1. Dan used mostly fastballs and sliders to come within four outs of our second no-hitter in twenty-three days, which would have been a dazzling final toast to an exceptional April. George Vukovich halted Petry's march to Cooperstown by lashing an outside fastball to left-center field for a two-out double in the eighth inning.

There were 24,853 delirious fans at this game, and they could have reacted with hostility when Vukovich's drive landed safely. Instead, they rose in unison and saluted Dan's effort with a standing ovation. I'll never forget Dan's response. He doffed his cap to demonstrate the strong bond of appreciation that exists between our fans and a team that is 18-2. We removed Dan after the eighth because he was physically and emotionally spent after his effort, which included three outstanding defensive plays by Tom Brookens. Dan realized the shallowness of a complete game under the circumstances. He agreed with the decision, realizing that Willie Hernandez needed an inning of work more than he needed a complete game. I am the choreographer of an entire staff, and have to prime Willie for the months ahead.

TIGERS 6, INDIANS 1   18 – 2

PITCHER	IP	H	R-ER	BB	SO	ERA
Petry (3-1)	8.0	1	0-0	2	7	2.06
Hernandez	1.0	1	1-1	1	1	4.86

WE'RE off today, but we packed enough into one month for a six-month expedition: a club-record nine victories at the season's outset and eighteen for the month, which ties a major league record; a 2.50 team earned run average; Jack Morris's no-hitter, the first by a Tiger since Jim Bunning's in 1958; and a six-game lead over our nearest rival, the Toronto Blue Jays.

I can't say enough about my pitching staff, but I tried. Call it my "Ode to April":

In April my staff was something to see,
With Jack Morris, the bullpen, and Dan Petry.
Jack was 5-0 with a no-hit game;
The last ball he threw to Kittle went to the Hall of Fame.
What was so great was that everybody on the staff had a win,
From all the starters to the fine bullpen.
Morris and Petry and all the other starters pitched well;
They even got compliments from Kaline and Kell.
There was Rozie, Berenguer, and Milt Wilcox—
They were the starters when we swept the White Sox.
Glenn Abbott pitched well and kept us in the game;
They call him the "Bowel Locker"—that's his nickname.
Also in the pen we have Doug Bair and Willie;
One's right and one's left and they can make you look silly.
And when we go to the ninth with the game on the line,
We call on Mr. Lopez, a favorite of mine.
Hernandez and Lopez make a fine pair,
But when they get in trouble we've always got Doug Bair.
Morris and Petry are my one-two punch,
But Berenguer, Wilcox, and Rozie—they ain't a bad bunch.
So as I look back on April when we were 18-2,
We battled rain, cold, snow, and also the flu,
But I'll always remember when I think back a little,
Jack Morris winding up and striking out Kittle.

TUESDAY, MAY 1   DETROIT

W E played an exhibition game for sandlot baseball last night in Cincinnati and brought up Dave Gumpert from our Triple-A affiliate in Evansville to pitch a few innings. Gumpert is a sometimes-fastidious youngster who did a good job for us last season and then fell victim to the spring training numbers game when we acquired Willie Hernandez. There are no soothing words for a person who was the club's rookie of the year last season and is presently beating the minor league bushes. I told him we are on a roll, but that the season is unpredictable. He has to keep working hard to climb back to the majors.

I had a similar experience in 1959, when the Los Angeles Dodgers sold my contract outright to Spokane of the Pacific Coast League. I had a bad arm, was placed on waivers, and was not claimed. Buzzie Bavasi of the Dodgers told me they couldn't carry damaged goods and pay a salary of $11,500. I was hurt but also determined. I vowed I'd be back within a month. He told me I would receive a $10,000 salary at Spokane and the $1,500 difference when I returned to the majors. I took him at his word and packed my Rambler station wagon. Carolyn was seven-and-a-half months pregnant. We drove 3,600 miles from Vero Beach, Florida, to Spokane, where I pitched the opening game and won. When Carl Erskine retired in June, I was recalled to Los Angeles and defeated the Cincinnati Reds, the same team I had beaten in my major league debut in 1955.

Buzzie shook my hand after the game and slipped me a $100 bill. He also made good on his promise. I finished the year with an 11-5 record and a 2.06 earned run average, which was far superior to that year's ERA champion—Sad Sam Jones at 2.89. I missed qualifying for that honor by one and one-third innings, but I felt a great sense of accomplishment after climbing from the low point to the high point of my professional career in the span of one season. Dave Gumpert and anyone else toiling in the obscurity of the minor leagues should bear that in mind. Minor league players who feel sorry for them-

I've worn a lot of uniforms in my day

selves won't enhance their chances of making it to the majors.

Milt Wilcox received a shot of cortisone a couple days ago and gave us eight strong innings today in an 11-2 pasting of the Boston Red Sox. Milt was loose and popping his fastball, which was running extremely well because he pulls down on the pitch with his middle finger and grips the ball a bit off-center. He could have notched a complete game, but why overexert any starting pitcher and risk injury?

TIGERS 11, RED SOX 2   19—2

PITCHER	IP	H	R-ER	BB	SO	ERA
Wilcox (3-0)	8.0	7	2-1	1	5	3.34
Lopez	1.0	1	0-0	0	1	1.33

WEDNESDAY, MAY 2   DETROIT

BASES on balls have always been a bane to pitchers. Juan Berenguer was a perfect example today. He issued five walks to the Boston Red Sox in six innings and got beat 5-4. Dwight Evans and Jim Rice followed two of Juan's walks with home runs.

Normally a pitcher will win a game when he pitches as well as Juan did today—he allowed only five base hits. Parrish and I try to steer Juan through games such as this one. Lance made several visits to the mound to remind Juan of some basics, such as keeping his eye on the glove target. I kept urging him to be more aggressive and challenge hitters instead of constantly falling behind in the count.

Juan does not have the consistency that our other starters have, but he's our scheduled fourth starter now. We did rebound with the authority of Moses Malone from a 5-0 deficit and left the tying run on second base in the ninth inning. I kept urging all the players on the bench to play this game as if it were the last game of the season because I know we're capable of quick comebacks.

Bob Stanley, Boston's formidable relief pitcher, demonstrated how to pitch backward. He threw Darrell Evans three straight palm balls—an off-speed pitch—after getting ahead in the count. Evans is a notorious fastball hitter, and Stanley's final palm ball was tapped to third baseman Wade Boggs for the second out of the ninth inning. Stanley then threw John Grubb a borderline full-count palm ball that Grubb took for a called third strike.

Stanley had us in the palm of his hand.

RED SOX 5, TIGERS 4   19 – 3

PITCHER	IP	H	R-ER	BB	SO	ERA
Berenguer (1-1)	6.0	5	5-5	5	3	2.61
Bair	2.0	2	0-0	0	3	1.59
Hernandez	1.0	1	0-0	0	1	4.58

THURSDAY, MAY 3   DETROIT

W E have a mild concern. Some of our players have been reporting late to the park. We do not want complacency. That could ruin our fine start. We reminded the players that we have a starting time. This is a good rule. When you have a regular job, your pay is docked if you're late. It's the same for this club. Tardiness carries a standard $100 fine. We hit at 5:15 before every home night game. If a player is not between the white lines at 5:15, Sparky wants a check for $100 to the guilty party's favorite charity on his desk the next day. This rule is a must. There are some clubs in the league that don't insist on such perfunctory habits. You won't win that way, regardless of your talent.

Jack Morris lost his first game and we dropped two in a row for the first time. Bob Ojeda and the Boston Red Sox beat us 1-0. Once again we had the tying run on second base with one out in the ninth inning, and once again the Red Sox stopped our rally. Jack pitched a strong game. Even in defeat he maintained his composure. Jack is prone to tantrums if he feels an umpire has made a bad call or if his teammates are not scoring runs for him.

Jack knew he had pitched well and deserved to win under normal circumstances. Ojeda had pitched an abnormally fine game.

RED SOX 1, TIGERS 0   19 — 4

PITCHER	IP	H	R-ER	BB	SO	ERA
Morris (5-1)	9.0	5	1-1	3	8	1.83

W E don't mind the solitary confinement this weekend. The attention we've been receiving has become something of a distraction. Our players are not accustomed to national acclaim. It seemed as if every reporter in America was in Detroit. Sparky even considered imposing a time limit on access to the clubhouse, making it a rule that no reporter could enter the clubhouse during the thirty minutes before game time. As it turned out, we didn't have to make any decision on the trip to Cleveland. Reporters aren't so interested in our story that they would follow us here.

We swept three games here. The games weren't pretty, but were wins nonetheless.

Our record of 22-4 will undoubtedly elicit more attention. We have a shot at the best thirty-game start in major league history (the 1955 Brooklyn Dodgers made it 25-5) and the most consecutive road victories with seventeen (the American League record is sixteen by the 1912 Washington Senators, and the major league mark is seventeen by the 1916 New York Giants). Those are long journeys into baseball's time tunnel. We welcome the trip.

Opening games often set the tone for a series by providing impetus for the remaining games. The first game here on Friday was no exception.

Petry struggled through five innings, battling his way through a performance in which his mechanics and his command of pitches were out of sync. He did escape a no-out, bases-loaded situation in the third inning without any damage, though, and brought us to a 5-2 lead after five innings before he was relieved. He had thrown more than one hundred pitches and had exerted himself a lot in that third inning.

Hernandez allowed just two hits over the final four innings for his third save. We broke the game open with three runs in the eighth inning. Willie's performance provides a perfect example of why we made sure he received an ample amount of work earlier.

Willie saved us in Cleveland

Friday, May 4

TIGERS 9, INDIANS 2   20 — 4

PITCHER	IP	H	R-ER	BB	SO	ERA
Petry (4-1)	5.0	6	2-2	6	5	2.25
Hernandez (S3)	4.0	2	0-0	1	3	3.74

Saturday, May 5

TIGERS 6, INDIANS 5   21 — 4

PITCHER	IP	H	R-ER	BB	SO	ERA
Abbott (2-1)	5.1	6	4-4	1	0	3.52
Bair	1.2	0	0-0	0	1	1.38
Lopez (S3)	2.0	3	1-1	0	3	1.61

Sunday, May 6

TIGERS 6, INDIANS 5 *(12 innings)*   22 — 4

PITCHER	IP	H	R-ER	BB	SO	ERA
Wilcox	5.0	8	5-4	3	5	3.89
Rozema	2.0	0	0-0	0	0	3.86
Hernandez	3.0	1	0-0	0	2	3.28
Lopez (3-0)	2.0	3	0-0	1	1	1.48

JUAN Berenguer opposed Mark Gubicza in a matchup of strong arms. We won 10-3 for our twelfth consecutive road victory. Our record is a 23-4 blur, which was being challenged by Gubicza's fastball. During the first three innings he registered six strikeouts.

Gubicza is an untrained rookie right-hander who stands six-foot-six, weighs 215 pounds, and turns twenty-two in August. Any pitching coach would love to get his hands on Mark. I was reminded of Juan those first three innings as Gubicza rushed fastballs past our hitters.

The trained pitcher prevailed. Gubicza suffered from a lack of any consistent off-speed pitch. He allowed five hits and a stolen base and walked three in the middle three innings for a yield of five runs. Juan pitched a strong game except for bad two-strike pitches to Frank White and Steve Balboni in a two-run Kansas City fourth inning. There is no question we were lucky here. The Royals were missing Willie Wilson and George Brett, both of whom will return to the lineup in one week.

Their absence gives us a distinct advantage. The Royals have no one on their bench to replace the speed of Wilson or the game-breaking bat of Brett.

TIGERS 10, ROYALS 3   23 — 4

PITCHER	IP	H	R-ER	BB	SO	ERA
Berenguer (2-1)	6.2	6	3-3	4	2	2.96
Bair (S2)	2.1	1	0-0	1	3	1.17

I try not to dwell on the past during the course of games. I also don't like to dwell on negatives. I did both here tonight.

Jack acted like a child scorned most of the evening. He pouted over a lack of run production on his behalf and a 2-0 deficit, kicking at the pitching mound and slamming down the resin bag.

In the dugout, I lectured Jack on my days with the New York Mets. I learned a lot about defeat and how to cope with adversity in 1963, when the Mets were shut out eleven times in games I started, including five 1-0 complete-game losses. I told Jack that when he's on the mound he cannot reveal his frustrations. Here's a guy who's supposed to be the best pitcher in baseball but who behaves like a little boy who's had his candy stolen. I was appalled by Jack's attitude and admonished him to do his job as well as possible, as hard as possible, and as long as possible. I guaranteed him that if he followed my advice a lot of good things would happen. The inspirational message didn't take affect. Jack had been beaten 1-0 by the Boston Red Sox in his previous start, and this game was beginning to look like an instant replay. Jack had fallen behind 1-0 when former Tiger farmhand Darryl Motley lashed a run-scoring single to right field in the fifth inning.

While we were batting in the sixth, Jack complained openly in the dugout about the lack of offensive support. "No one wants to play behind you when you act like this," Parrish bluntly told him. In the bottom of the sixth Jack surrendered a solo home run to Jorge Orta. Trammell then went to the mound and encouraged Jack to hang tough, pointing out that the club had rallied before. Jack retired the final twelve batters and Trammell rewarded him with a grand slam home run. A 5-2 win over Dan Quisenberry became another chapter in our Walter Mitty season. After the game, Jack credited Parrish and Trammell with helping him realize what a jerk he was on this particular evening.

The years I spent with Casey Stengel's Amazin' Mets were frustrating, but all those shutout losses translated into one victory twenty-one years later.

TIGERS 5, ROYALS 2   24 – 4

PITCHER	IP	H	R-ER	BB	SO	ERA
Morris (6-1)	9.0	7	2-2	2	5	1.85

T HE telephone is my alarm clock. It rings incessantly because we are within one victory of establishing the record
for the best thirty-game start in major league history.

The 1955 Brooklyn Dodgers, a club I joined in July, won
twenty-five of their first thirty games. We are 25-4 after strong
pitching from Dan Petry and Aurelio Lopez swept us past the
Kansas City Royals 3-1 tonight. One guy from New York even
asked me how I felt to be associated with the two greatest
teams in baseball history. I applied the brakes out of respect
for standouts such as Pee Wee Reese, Gil Hodges, Jackie Robinson, Roy Campanella, Carl Furillo, Duke Snider, Don Newcombe, and Carl Erskine. We had a lot of all-stars on that '55
team, and we're going to have four or five this year from the
Tigers. There's not a lot of difference except the Dodgers had
more experience.

The best measure of the two clubs is their high professional standard. The Dodgers expected to win, and if they lost
they still expected to win the next day. There was no back
slapping or hand shaking. They were the Boys of Summer who
were saddled with frustration every October by their cross-town
rival the New York Yankees until 1955, when Brooklyn claimed
its only World Championship.

I will never forget that World Series. I warmed up in the
bullpen each of the first four games, a rookie pitcher who felt
like a wild stallion ready to bust out of a corral. About the
middle of the fourth game, manager Walter Alston called the
bullpen and told pitching coach Joe Becker to sit me down. I
was disturbed because I was itching for action. After the game,
which we won to tie the Series at two games apiece, Alston
took me aside and asked me how I felt. I told him I felt great.
He said that was good because I was his choice to start the
pivotal fifth game the next day. If I had jumped into a pool of
water I would have been electrocuted. I felt like 50,000 volts of
energy was shooting through my body.

Alston didn't regret his decision. We won the fifth game 5-3. I pitched six innings for the victory, with a save from Clem Labine. We went on to win the championship in seven games.

I'll never forget the clubhouse atmosphere after the final World Series game. I had a championship ring and a full World Series share after half a season in the major leagues. Guys such as Furillo, Robinson, Reese, Snider, Hodges, and Campanella were even more emotional. The spirit of that club was built on hard work and frustration, and when they realized what they had done they broke down and wept unashamedly in front of their lockers.

Kirk Gibson was asked his recollections of Furillo, his right field counterpart on the Dodgers. "Did I go to high school with him?" Kirk asked.

TIGERS 3, ROYALS 1   25 – 4

PITCHER	IP	H	R-ER	BB	SO	ERA
Petry (5-1)	6.2	7	1-1	4	5	2.12
Lopez (S4)	2.1	0	0-0	1	4	1.35

Gibby never heard of Carl Furillo

FRIDAY, MAY 11   DETROIT

J IMMY Russo, the superscout for the World Champion Baltimore Orioles, showed up here tonight and wondered when
we're going to let the rest of the East Division up for air. Play
.500 baseball, Russo said, and you can be assured of a fine
season. Maybe Russo didn't know that the Tigers had won 106
of our past 164 games spanning two seasons. That's a .646
winning clip, or 104 victories in one season.

We won our seventh straight game 8-2 over the California
Angels to improve our record to 26-4 and succeed the 1955
Brooklyn Dodgers as the team to post the best thirty-game
start in baseball history. There were 44,000 fans on hand and
they gave us a standing ovation prior to the game. Our players
appreciate this type of enthusiasm, but I don't think they are
obsessed with records. I believe one secret to our success is
that the club has a single goal—the World Series. Records are
merely a by-product of that goal. The record meant more to
me because I've already been in four Series. I still wear a World
Championship ring on each hand.

I had a conference with Milt Wilcox before the game and
told him to quit working the corners of the plate so much. This
results in walks. He gave up only one in six innings before
Sparky replaced him because he had a little tenderness in his
pitching elbow.

TIGERS 8, ANGELS 2   26 — 4

PITCHER	IP	H	R-ER	BB	SO	ERA
Wilcox (4-0)	6.0	6	0-0	1	5	3.32
Hernandez (S4)	3.0	4	2-2	0	0	3.58

SATURDAY, MAY 12   DETROIT

N OT many people upstage a monster home run by Reggie Jackson on national television. Sparky tried today.

Sparky became incensed over a runner's interference call made by second base umpire Ted Hendry in the ninth inning of our 4-2 loss to the California Angels. Hendry's call proved correct, which Sparky later admitted, but he argued for ten minutes to blunt the memory of Reggie's sixth-inning homer over the right-field roof off Juan Berenguer. Managers will occasionally spar verbally with umpires in an attempt to ignite their club, especially when the club is in a losing rut. Sparky also hoped to upset the rhythm of Angels' pitcher Tommy John, who went the distance. John is a veteran, but sometimes you can get under the skin of a pitcher by staging a prolonged debate with an umpire. You also can stimulate a reaction in a large partisan crowd, which can work favorably for your club.

Sparky lost the call and we lost the game.

ANGELS 4, TIGERS 2   26 — 5

PITCHER	IP	H	R-ER	BB	SO	ERA
Berenguer (2-2)	6.2	10	3-3	3	6	3.18
Lopez	2.1	1	1-1	0	0	1.55

BASES on balls are a pitching coach's nightmare. I've been hammering this point home to Wilcox. Too often he attempts to make perfect pitches instead of challenging hitters. A pitcher shouldn't give a hitter too much credit. A baseball isn't that easy to hit.

The Seattle Mariners helped me make my point by issuing twelve walks in the middle game of our three-game sweep. Five of those twelve walks contributed to our six runs. Milt had apparently paid attention. He issued only two free passes in six innings as we completed a sweep to run our record to 29-5.

Monday, May 14
TIGERS 7, MARINERS 5   27 – 5

PITCHER	IP	H	R-ER	BB	SO	ERA
Petry	5.0	6	3-3	2	1	2.44
Bair	2.0	1	2-2	2	1	2.08
Lopez (4-0)	2.0	2	0-0	0	1	1.45

Tuesday, May 15
TIGERS 6, MARINERS 4   28 – 5

PITCHER	IP	H	R-ER	BB	SO	ERA
Morris (7-1)	7.0	3	4-3	5	4	2.04
Hernandez (S5)	2.0	2	0-0	1	5	3.34

Wednesday, May 16
TIGERS 10, MARINERS 1   29 – 5

PITCHER	IP	H	R-ER	BB	SO	ERA
Wilcox (5-0)	6.0	4	1-1	2	5	3.09
Bair	1.0	1	0-0	0	0	1.96
Hernandez	1.0	0	0-0	0	0	3.23
Lopez	1.0	1	0-0	0	1	1.41

RICK Dempsey is a spunky catcher for the Baltimore Orioles. He made some pugnacious remarks about the Tigers to Larry King, the syndicated columnist and talk-show host. Dempsey said the Tigers are a good team but not a great team, and that Jack Morris is odds-on to lose three or four more games if he loses one tough one. My guess is that Rick is trying to distract us. The Orioles are ten and one-half games behind and haven't enjoyed the type of hoopla generally accorded a World Championship team. Media people thrive on controversial statements. Players realize this and sometimes attempt to use it to their advantage. We must be careful what we say in front of reporters. Their interpretation of our words can differ from what we meant. In baseball, we are not all English majors.

Our players read Dempsey's comments in the local papers. We encouraged them to keep a low profile. Jack responded admirably. He thanked Mr. Dempsey for his remarks, noting that they would further inspire the Tigers. It showed that he is capable of handling negative barbs. That makes this off-day and the entire incident worthwhile.

RICK Dempsey recanted. The Tigers did not. We swept a three-game series with the Oakland A's.

In the clubhouse, you can't detect whether we've won or lost—and we're 32-5! I don't believe the players realize the significance of their accomplishments.

Dempsey now maintains he never told Baltimore-area reporters Jack Morris was overrated, and he says that the Tigers are a great team. Once again Jack stayed out of the verbal boxing ring, saying only that players sometimes are misquoted, and that he has a great deal of respect for the Orioles.

We played this series without Sparky Anderson, who returned to California for the funeral of his father, LeRoy. I missed the Sunday game to attend the twentieth reunion of the 1964 World Champion St. Louis Cardinals. There was a lot of time to reminisce with such people as Curt Flood, Dick Groat, Lou Brock, Mike Shannon, Ron Taylor, Julian Javier, and Bob Uecker, who was my roommate. The wives voted me the player who had changed the least. I asked Diane Sadecki, the wife of pitcher Ray Sadecki, if that meant I looked this old twenty years ago. Everybody laughed.

Ron Taylor, Ken Boyer, and I celebrate the 1964 championship

Home on the range

Carolyn and I spent the off-day on Monday at our home near San Diego. I rode Old Amos, a gaited horse, and stumbled across a five-foot rattlesnake. I rolled a log over the snake, borrowed a shovel from some guys working on the road, and cut off the rattler's head. As a prank, I wrapped the snake in an old shirt and gave it to Carolyn as a present. She ran screaming into the house.

Friday, May 18
TIGERS 8, A's 4 *(5 innings)*   30 − 5

PITCHER	IP	H	R-ER	BB	SO	ERA
Petry (6-1)	5.1	7	4-4	2	4	2.84

Saturday, May 19
TIGERS 5, A's 4   31 − 5

PITCHER	IP	H	R-ER	BB	SO	ERA
Morris (8-1)	7.1	8	3-3	6	6	2.19
Lopez (S5)	1.2	1	1-1	0	0	1.60

Sunday, May 20
TIGERS 4, A's 3   32 − 5

PITCHER	IP	H	R-ER	BB	SO	ERA
Wilcox (6-0)	6.0	3	2-2	1	0	3.08
Hernandez (S6)	3.0	1	1-1	0	2	3.21

W E established an American League record for most consecutive road victories—seventeen—while tying the National League mark in a three-game sweep of California.

Columbus didn't enjoy this much success on the road.

Our record is 35-5, the best forty-game start in the history of baseball. We even received a standing ovation from an Anaheim Stadium crowd of 43,580 in the ninth inning of the final game of the series.

Morris struck out ten in a 5-1 victory to bump his record to 9-1 and move twelve days ahead of Denny McLain's thirty-one victory pace for the Tigers in 1968. Jack has a chance at thirty victories. He's a superior athlete who never misses a turn. He also believes he's the best pitcher in baseball. Right now he is. Glenn Abbott claims that a scouting report submitted by Phil Regan of the Seattle Mariners said the only person who can beat Jack is God.

Jack wasn't the sole reason I popped my buttons. We allowed only four runs in the three games, and one of those was unearned. Berenguer struck out nine in six innings in the opener, including Reggie with a 2-2 split-fingered fastball to close out the sixth.

Reggie, who cleared the Tiger Stadium roof at Juan's expense ten days earlier, resorted to mind games by motioning for Juan to throw him a thigh-high pitch. But Reggie couldn't touch the split-finger. The next day he approached our dugout before the game. He told me he didn't know much about pitching coaches and didn't like them because they conspire to get him out, but he complimented me on Juan's progress. Those words from a future Hall of Famer will stick with me a long time.

The last day in Anaheim a reporter for ESPN, the sports television network, asked me about reports circulating in Southern California concerning my possible managerial prospects for next season. No one has contacted me and I'd prefer not to think about the possibility, although I'm not sure what I'd do if someone offered me a job. Carolyn wants me to retire this fall. My long-time friend John McNamara, who manages the Angels, gave me every reason to stay in Detroit when he told me after the game that he couldn't remember seeing any team in seventeen years play as well as we're playing.

Tuesday, May 22
TIGERS 3, ANGELS 1   33 – 5

PITCHER	IP	H	R-ER	BB	SO	ERA
Berenguer (3-2)	6.0	3	1-1	3	9	2.93
Lopez (S6)	3.0	2	0-0	1	4	1.47

Wednesday, May 23
TIGERS 4, ANGELS 2   34 – 5

PITCHER	IP	H	R-ER	BB	SO	ERA
Petry (7-1)	7.0	5	2-2	2	5	2.81
Hernandez (S7)	2.0	0	0-0	0	3	3.03

Thursday, May 24
TIGERS 5, ANGELS 1   35 – 5

PITCHER	IP	H	R-ER	BB	SO	ERA
Morris (9-1)	9.0	4	1-0	1	10	1.97

BRUSHBACK and knockdown pitches are becoming less commonplace because umpires intercede much more quickly these days and because there is no possibility of personal retaliation against the pitcher in the designated-hitter league. More and more hitters are leaning over the plate to take the outside corner away from pitchers, who have to pitch to the middle of the plate and in to be effective. I personally think it's too bad if a batter gets hit crowding the plate. I know that Don Drysdale, Larry Sherry, and Stan Williams felt the same way when they pitched for the Dodgers in the late 1950s and early '60s. That was the formula I was raised on. Come to think of it, I've never seen a batter apologize for smashing a line drive off some part of a pitcher's torso.

The Seattle Mariners brushed back Lance Parrish, Larry Herndon, and Kirk Gibson—while sweeping us three games. It was time some team demonstrated a little defiance of a 35-5 club. We have some pitchers who are not against retaliatory measures—most notably Wilcox, but this series didn't lend itself to hardball rebuttals. Our pitching staff was hammered for twenty-two runs and thirty-seven hits in twenty-four innings, but there is no cause for alarm. The rude treatment we experienced here is an everyday occurrence for some staffs. We will not be dominant in each of our 162 games. My job is to analyze the problem and make necessary corrections. The biggest pitching problem in this series was a failure to get ahead in the count, resulting in a heavy reliance on fastballs. You can't trick hitters when you're constantly pitching from behind.

Two other factors made Seattle a pain for us—artificial turf and a dome. I don't like domes and I especially don't like phony turf because ground balls that normally would be outs scoot through for base hits. The Kingdome, like the Metrodome in Minneapolis, is a hitter's paradise. Being here deepens my appreciation for Tiger Stadium, where the grass is allowed to reach a reasonable length, so it slows down ground balls and helps our pitchers. Sure, our hitters are going to be robbed of some base hits by the grass in the Tiger infield, too, but we are essentially a home-run-hitting team, and there is no defense for a home run. On the other hand, our use of the split-fingered fastball, which breaks down when thrown properly, should result in an abundance of ground balls by the opposition. Many of those will be devoured by the Tiger Stadium grass.

This weekend was so bleak that Rusty Kuntz submitted a check to the coaches as a fine for being picked off base twice in Anaheim. We declined. This is no time to accentuate negative thoughts. We have to dwell on the positive. Right now that is the most important thing.

In the aftermath of this series, Alex Grammas, our third base coach, recalled one knockdown incident he was involved in. The culprit was Jim Hughes, a burly, beer-drinking pitcher for the Brooklyn Dodgers. Alex was in the on-deck circle when the late Ken Boyer, third base standout of the St. Louis Cardinals, drilled a home run off Hughes. When Brooklyn manager Walter Alston bounded out of the dugout to remove Hughes from the game, Grammas, fearing a fastball to his ribs, heaved a sigh of relief. But when Alston asked for the ball, Hughes turned and threw at Grammas. In the old days pitchers even knocked down hitters in the on-deck circle!

Friday, May 25
MARINERS 7, TIGERS 3   35 — 6

PITCHER	IP	H	R-ER	BB	SO	ERA
Wilcox (6-1)	4.2	9	6-5	2	1	3.61
Bair	1.1	1	1-1	0	1	2.33
Rozema	1.0	1	0-0	0	1	3.64
Abbott	1.0	1	0-0	0	0	3.31

Sparky and Alex Grammas have worked together for eleven years

Saturday, May 26

MARINERS 9, TIGERS 5   35 – 7

PITCHER	IP	H	R-ER	BB	SO	ERA
Berenguer (3-3)	0.1	5	4-4	1	0	3.79
Bair	3.2	2	1-1	1	3	2.31
Rozema	2.0	2	2-1	2	1	3.72
Abbott	1.0	2	2-2	0	0	4.15
Hernandez	1.0	0	0-0	0	0	2.95

Sunday, May 27

MARINERS 6, TIGERS 1   35 – 8

PITCHER	IP	H	R-ER	BB	SO	ERA
Petry (7-2)	4.0	9	4-2	1	4	2.91
Lopez	4.0	5	2-2	1	3	1.77

JACK Morris ended our losing streak, and Steve Boros jarred my memory. Boros was fired as manager of the Oakland A's, the team Jack defeated, 6-2, to run his record to 10-1. Managing is a fickle form of employment. I tried it once with the San Diego Padres, lasted two years in 1978-79, and got fired in San Francisco on the final day of the 1979 season.

Ballard Smith, who still serves as president of the Padres, called me to his room to meet with him and general manager Bob Fontaine. The news hurt deeply. I had managed the Padres to eighty-four victories in 1978, the most in club history, but we had fallen off to only sixty-seven wins entering the final game of the '79 season against the Giants. I reminded Smith and Fontaine that an arm injury had reduced the number of saves recorded by Rollie Fingers from thirty-seven to twelve, but my argument was in vain. They asked me to manage that final game (which we won 3-2), and when I took the lineup card to home plate, Dave Bristol, the Giants' manager, asked about my situation for the following season. When I told him I was fired, he was incredulous. (One year later, he was fired himself.)

I still maintain that a mid-season discussion with Smith and Fontaine cost me my job. I urged them to make several trades. But Fontaine, who previously had served as scouting director and thus was instrumental in developing most of the Padres players, didn't support my suggestion. Ironically, there isn't a single player on the 1984 Padres who was there at the time I was fired.

Jack went the distance here for his seventh complete game. He has now pitched one hundred and one-third innings, a heavy workload, but I don't think he has been overworked. He's pitched on the fourth or fifth day along with the rest of our starting pitchers. Furthermore he relishes the endurance role and considers it the ultimate challenge for a quality pitcher. Steve Carlton, whom Jack idolizes, has pitched in the vicinity of three hundred innings per season for several years, and Carlton is thirty-nine years old.

We lost the second game of this series after Wilcox became riled at home plate umpire Steve Palermo, who ejected Milt from a game last season. Some umpires seem to work against certain players; this can result from a personality clash or words that were exchanged earlier. In this instance, I sided with Milt, but there's precious little that can be done to rectify the situation. Milt feels defeated before the game even begins if Palermo is the home plate umpire; we can only hope he's umpiring the bases when Milt is on the mound.

We did capture the third game on a home run by Gibson and fine relief pitching from Hernandez and Lopez. Willie replaced Juan Berenguer in the fifth inning after Juan walked Carney Lansford with the bases loaded to force home the first run of the game. Sparky and I felt it was imperative to prevent any more runs if we were to win. The prospects of scoring runs off Oakland starter Steve McCatty were not good, and a three- or four-run inning by the A's would have been fatal. Willie did the job for three and one-third scoreless innings, and Lopez registered his seventh save to stamp Gibson's ninth-inning homer as the game-winning RBI.

Gibson seems to thrive on pressure. He's a born winner who has begun to assume a leadership role. He'll jump on players once in a while if he thinks they're not playing their hardest—that happened in the final game when Gibson admonished the team in general to reach for reserve strength. Every club periodically needs someone to motivate it—a role filled by Enos Cabell last season. If someone wasn't hustling, Cabell would tell him to take off his uniform if he didn't want to play. He was a leader for us, and I wish we still had him.

Monday, May 28
TIGERS 6, A's 2   36 − 8

PITCHER	IP	H	R-ER	BB	SO	ERA
Morris (10-1)	9.0	7	2-1	0	8	1.88

Tuesday, May 29
A's 8, TIGERS 5   36 − 9

PITCHER	IP	H	R-ER	BB	SO	ERA
Wilcox (6-2)	3.1	7	7-7	3	1	4.45
Bair	1.2	4	1-1	0	0	2.52
Rozema	2.0	2	0-0	2	1	3.38
Hernandez	1.0	1	0-0	0	1	2.87

Wednesday, May 30
TIGERS 2, A's 1   37 − 9

PITCHER	IP	H	R-ER	BB	SO	ERA
Berenguer	4.2	2	1-0	4	2	3.40
Hernandez (2-0)	3.1	2	0-0	2	2	2.63
Lopez (S7)	1.0	0	0-0	0	0	1.73

I can't allow the month of May to slip away without another tribute to my staff. They won nineteen of twenty-six games and posted an earned run average of 3.14.

> In the month of May we were 19-7,
> Morris, Petry, and Wilcox won a total of 11.
> We broke the record for wins on the road,
> Bair, Lopez, and Hernandez carried the load.
> Morris won five, and Petry chalked up four,
> And when things got tough Willie and Lopey
>   slammed the door.
> Rozie and Abbott didn't pitch a lot,
> That's what happens when your starters are hot.
> We also broke the '55 Brooklyn Dodgers' record of 25-4,
> The starters pitched well, and so did the relief corps.
> Jack Morris's record at this point is 10-1,
> He'll be something to see when he's all done.
> Petry is 7-2 and learning all the time,
> He'll be super to see when he reaches his prime.
> Wilcox is 6-2 and having trouble with his split-finger,
> He's pitching okay, but throwing up an occasional dinger.
> Lest we forget Mr. Juan Berenguer,
> As well as he's pitched, he gives Sparky a scare.
> His split-finger may not take him to the Hall of Fame,
> But when he struck out Reggie it won him the game.
> Doug Bair keeps waiting to do his thing,
> But come August you may see his arm in a sling.
> I can't say enough about Lopey and Willie,
> One is healthy and the other, he ain't in Philly.
> As a coach you like to see more work from Rozie and Abby,
> But at this point the staff isn't too shabby.
> So as we go into June 37-9,
> Those pitchers I have are one of a kind.

THE Orioles arrived ten and one-half games off our pace and abruptly lost another. We prevailed 14-2 behind a robust offense and six shutout innings from Dan Petry.

There has been a great deal of sniping aimed at us by Rick Dempsey and Ken Singleton, and the atmosphere is electric. I could barely see the players through the horde of reporters in our clubhouse. A gentleman from my hometown of Durham, North Carolina, even appeared to do an article on me. The attention, I think, is interesting. This series offers a World Series excitement, and Detroit provides good copy for reporters such as Larry Guest, the sports editor of *The Orlando Sentinel.* "Sure, this is premature," he said, "but so

Petry clipped the Orioles' wings

what? It's fun and healthy. Why act oversophisticated and wait until August and September? I think this city will have fun then, too." We have energized not only the city of Detroit but the entire baseball world in a year that was supposed to be the sole property of the Olympic Games.

Not everyone is rooting for us, of course. We're ruining the summer for a lot of fans and members of the media who want tight pennant races. Consider the newspaper death notices bestowed upon us in Seattle when we were 35-7: "Tigers for real, or will they go up in smoke?"—and in Chicago when we were 36-9: "Tigers still floundering."

The Tiger doubters were fortified when Baltimore defeated us the final two games of the series to move to within nine and one-half games. Storm Davis outpitched Morris, 5-0, in the second game, and Mike Flanagan beat Wilcox, 2-1, in the third game. I was disappointed we didn't win the series after so convincingly claiming the first game, but I'm not discouraged. When you lead the reigning World Champions by nine and one-half games, you're doing something right.

Sparky and I decided it would be best to go to a five-man starting rotation. Guys like Morris and Petry are going to need this rest now so that the hot months of August and September won't drain us. There is a mental drain that must be avoided, too. Dan and Milt aren't affected as much as Jack, because Jack pitches more innings. Pitching every fifth day, rather than every fourth day, will allow Jack to be stronger physically and mentally over a longer period. I also think my bullpen is going to be the difference down the stretch. I have the best relief staff of any club with Hernandez, Lopez, Bair, and Rozema. Dan Quisenberry might be better than Lopez, and Tippy Martinez, some say, is better than Willie. We'll see.

Friday, June 1
TIGERS 14, ORIOLES 2   38 – 9

PITCHER	IP	H	R-ER	BB	SO	ERA
Petry (8-2)	6.0	3	0-0	1	1	2.68
Bair (S3)	3.0	4	2-2	0	3	2.89

Saturday, June 2

ORIOLES 5, TIGERS 0   38 – 10

PITCHER	IP	H	R-ER	BB	SO	ERA
Morris (10-2)	6.0	7	5-5	1	1	2.20
Hernandez	1.2	2	0-0	1	3	2.53
Lopez	1.1	0	0-0	0	2	1.67

Sunday, June 3

ORIOLES 2, TIGERS 1   38 – 11

PITCHER	IP	H	R-ER	BB	SO	ERA
Wilcox (6-3)	5.2	4	2-1	6	4	4.21
Rozema	3.1	1	0-0	1	3	2.92

Tom Brookens' first home run of the season wasn't enough to defeat Baltimore

W E won three of seven games from the Baltimore Orioles and Toronto Blue Jays—splitting a four-game set with the Jays, who arrived trailing us by four and one-half games and departed at the same distance. I'm sure some people were disappointed in the split, but I think it's important to remember that Toronto came to Tiger Stadium with fifteen wins in its previous nineteen games, while we had lost six of our previous nine. Every time we looked around, Toronto was winning. No matter how well we played, they were still on our heels. In the recesses of my mind I fear they could catch us.

The split was a showcase of each club's ace starting pitcher—Dave Stieb of the Blue Jays and Morris. Stieb had a 3-0 lead in the seventh inning of the series opener, but he lost it on a three-run home run by Howard Johnson. We finally triumphed, 6-3, in ten innings after one of the fiercest pitcher-batter confrontations I have ever witnessed: Dave Bergman fouled off seven two-strike pitches from Roy Lee Jackson and then culminated a seven-minute at-bat by drilling a full-count delivery for a three-run homer. This was baseball in its simplest and purest form: Jackson, the pitcher, against Bergman, the hitter; first place team against second place team; tenth inning of a tied game; two outs and two runners on base.

The clubhouse went crazy. There were between fifty and sixty reporters in our clubhouse, which is one of the smallest in the league, and four television mini-cameras converged on Bergman's locker. We had beaten the club that had been gaining on us, the dramatic victory seeming even larger after Toronto claimed the next two games, 8-4 and 6-3, to pull within three and one-half games.

Jack restored order in the fourth game, 5-3, as a new Tiger was born. Ruppert Jones, whose contract was purchased from Evansville, delivered a three-run home run to break a 1-1 tie, and Jack gamely preserved the lead by going the distance for the eighth time. Jack is now leading the league in strikeouts, wins, innings pitched . . . and confidence. We made our second roster change of the season by purchasing right-handed relief pitcher Carl Willis from Evansville. Jones and Willis replaced catcher Dwight Lowry and outfielder Rod Allen. I always hate to see a player sent to the minor leagues; that's the toughest phase of coaching because there's a big difference between the majors and the minors in terms of salary, attention, living conditions, and business opportunities. But all teams must be concerned with strengthening their lineup. Not only will some players be sent to the minors, but most players will be traded during the course of their career—trades are an occupational hazard. Players come to expect transactions, and don't necessarily regret leaving a team—at least the new team wants their talents.

Willis made my trip to the Instructional League in St. Petersburg, Florida, last winter worthwhile. He kept all his pitches low in the strike zone, and we decided to take him to spring training as a nonroster player. He almost made the club. Carl is going to be outstanding; he doesn't pitch scared. I'll never forget what he told me in spring training after he first threw batting practice. When I asked him how he felt, he said he was nervous. I shrugged that off and offered reassurance by telling him he had thrown strikes. "Aw, I can always throw strikes," he responded. That impressed me. The kid didn't have one year of pro ball under his belt, but he did have some swagger. Of course, he was raised in North Carolina.

My own first trip to the majors was a longer journey than from Evansville, Indiana, to Detroit. I was playing for the Montreal Royals and we were in Havana, Cuba. Tom Lasorda, now the manager of the Los Angeles Dodgers, and I had pitched our club to a doubleheader sweep. The next morning I was summoned to see my manager, Greg Mullevy. "You know you're going to pitch Sunday," he said. "Yes, you told me that," I replied. I was a bit piqued that I'd gotten up early for this. Then he told me I would be pitching in Brooklyn for the Dodgers. I nearly fainted.

Monday, June 4
TIGERS 6, BLUE JAYS 3 *(10 innings)*   39 – 11

PITCHER	IP	H	R-ER	BB	SO	ERA
Berenguer	6.2	8	3-3	2	7	3.48
Hernandez	3.0	2	0-0	1	3	2.36
Lopez (5-0)	0.1	0	0-0	0	0	1.66

Tuesday, June 5
BLUE JAYS 8, TIGERS 4   39 – 12

PITCHER	IP	H	R-ER	BB	SO	ERA
Abbott (2-2)	3.1	6	5-5	0	0	5.66
Bair	3.0	4	3-3	1	3	3.48
Rozema	2.2	1	0-0	1	1	2.63

Wednesday, June 6
BLUE JAYS 6, TIGERS 3   39 – 13

PITCHER	IP	H	R-ER	BB	SO	ERA
Petry (8-3)	4.0	10	5-5	0	0	3.12
Lopez	4.0	2	1-1	2	2	1.71
Hernandez	1.0	1	0-0	0	1	2.31

Thursday, June 7
TIGERS 5, BLUE JAYS 3   40 – 13

PITCHER	IP	H	R-ER	BB	SO	ERA
Morris (11-2)	9.0	7	3-1	1	4	2.11

W E expected to be badgered in Baltimore, but not by the police. Sparky Anderson and I were walking near the beautiful inner harbor. The weather was hot and muggy, and we were without shirts. An officer stopped to advise us that there is an ordinance against walking without shirts. I assured him we would take our sweat somewhere else, but Sparky became a bit annoyed and started to protest until I told him it wouldn't look good in the papers if we were arrested because we refused to wear shirts.

Sparky takes a walk virtually every day for the physical exercise; I accompany him about half the time for mental exercise. We discuss every aspect of the team, including possible trades. I have one pet peeve with Sparky: I'm a Barbaro Garbey man and think we should find a position for him every day. I think Garbey is one of the best pure hitters on the club, but Sparky isn't sure Garbey can play every day and likes his value as a utility player off the bench. This boils down to one thing: Sparky just doesn't like Garbey as a player as much as I do. We will keep walking and I'll keep talking. The days when I don't walk with Sparky I swim laps in our hotel pool. This is where I have an advantage on Sparky: he can't swim.

I held a meeting with my pitchers prior to the game and emphasized the advantage of pitching inside more frequently. A couple of our pitchers have shied away from this, especially Dan Petry, and it has been reflected in their performance. Ask any hitter the toughest pitch to hit when he has two strikes, and he'll tell you the good, hard fastball inside. Hitters are trying to protect the plate and make contact. Some hitters still make the mistake of swinging for home runs when they're behind in the count. The inside fastball doesn't allow home run hitters to extend their arms and get maximum power into their swing. Hernandez, Lopez, and Morris use the inside fastball efficiently, and Hernandez put on a clinic tonight, pitching two scoreless innings as we defeated the Orioles, 3-2.

People marvel at Willie's screwball, but the reason for its effectiveness is that Willie knows how to pitch inside and has the fastball to do so. The pitching pattern of fastball inside and screwball away is simple and yet exceedingly tough on right-handed hitters, who are never fully prepared to reach out for Willie's screwball. In the back of their minds they know Willie can buzz them inside with his fastball. Milt Wilcox, who pitched six innings and received credit for the victory, used his fastball well, too, and Doug Bair continued to perform his statistically thankless job with one scoreless inning in advance of Willie.

The Orioles tried several measures to fluster us. They distributed "Tiger Tails," their version of the Pittsburgh Steelers' "Terrible Towels," prior to the game and adopted the rather infantile slogan "Catch a Tiger by the tail." Our players had advance warning of this through the media, and the Baltimore tactic had no bearing on our performance. Baltimore also took the liberty of playing the original Motown rendition of "Dancin' in the Streets" at the conclusion of the fifth inning. Tiger management has refused to play that song at Tiger Stadium despite pressure from one of the Detroit papers to do so. The media's criticism of management policies occupies very little of our time. Some players, such as Jack Morris, are a bit amused because Jack has been lobbying for a new sound system for a long time.

We now have won the opening game of nineteen of the twenty-one series we've played to date—another extraordinary statistic in an extraordinary season.

TIGERS 3, ORIOLES 2   41 – 13

PITCHER	IP	H	R-ER	BB	SO	ERA
Wilcox (7-3)	6.0	4	2-2	2	1	4.11
Bair	1.0	0	0-0	0	1	3.38
Hernandez (S8)	2.0	2	0-0	1	2	2.22

BERENGUER demonstrated today that he is more sensitive to his feelings than to line drives to his skull. He was struck above his right ear by a line drive off the bat of Al Bumbry in the third inning, but he remained in the game and battled gallantly until we removed him in the sixth inning because of leg cramps. Juan trailed, 1-0, when he departed and we lost, 4-0. He was disconsolate and frustrated afterward because he had wanted to stay in the game. He wants so badly to succeed and we haven't scored a single run for him in his past three

Juan is a sensitive—and serious—pitcher

starts. I have to bolster his confidence. No one is intentionally refusing to score runs when he's on the mound, but still he seems to wallow in self-pity.

He requested a meeting in Sparky's office after the game at which I was present as were Willie Hernandez and Aurelio Lopez, who served as interpreters. This was bizarre! Juan believes he is being followed and that his family is threatened. He has some unfounded suspicions that the club is having him tailed. While I don't actually believe for one moment that he is being tailed, I'm sure he feels his assumptions are true. I don't take them seriously and feel they will pass when he shakes his insecurity. I told Juan no one in our organization would ever interfere with his private life. I offered to help him, but told him I would not follow him into bars or restaurants. I'm not a detective or a baby-sitter. Maybe he misinterpreted a gaze from an admiring fan who recognized him. The league does police players who have alcohol or drug problems, but this does not apply to Juan.

I had a good meeting with Dan Petry prior to the game. I want to reinforce his confidence in his fastball because the word is getting around the league that he's relying too much on his slider. This is hurting him, especially on two-strike pitches. Dan was very receptive; as I've said before, he's very coachable and always willing to listen without being offended.

ORIOLES 4, TIGERS 0   41 — 14

PITCHER	IP	H	R-ER	BB	SO	ERA
Berenguer (3-4)	5.1	3	2-2	4	6	3.47
Lopez	0.1	3	2-2	1	0	2.08
Willis	2.1	1	0-0	1	0	0.00

SUNDAY, JUNE 10   BALTIMORE

THIS was our "seven-eleven" day. We swept a doubleheader from the Baltimore Orioles by scores of 10-4 and 8-0 to move seven games ahead of the Toronto Blue Jays and eleven ahead of the Orioles. We played for a split by starting Abbott against their ace Mike Boddicker in the opener, while saving Petry to go against Dennis Martinez in the nightcap. Our players dismissed that strategy, especially Lou Whitaker, Alan Trammell, and Kirk Gibson, who combined for fourteen hits, nine runs, and eleven RBIs.

Glenn understood our thinking. He's been around baseball long enough to recognize our reasons for safeguarding a split, and he considered the assignment a challenge. He went to the mound to prove Sparky and me wrong. Unfortunately, he didn't get out of the third inning; we won with our bats and stellar relief from Doug Bair, who recorded his five hundredth major league strikeout, and Willie Hernandez. My greatest satisfaction came from Petry, who shut out the Orioles on three hits in the second game. He was aggressive and kept coming at the Orioles to run his string of scoreless innings against them to fifteen.

There was an altercation between Dan and Lance Parrish early in the game that began in our dugout and extended into the clubhouse. Dan became miffed at Lance, who had some signs for fastballs shaken off in the first few innings. Lance pouted and, in effect, told Dan to do it his own way. Cool heads did not prevail; there was a lot of shouting and screaming, which is a bit uncommon for a team in first place and on its way to a sweep of the reigning World Champions. I interceded and emphasized to Dan and Lance that they have to work together. But the outburst may have been healthy therapy; Dan and Lance shook hands after the game as if nothing had happened.

COURTESY THE GRAND RAPIDS PRESS

A shouting match between Petry and Parrish resulted in victory

TIGERS 10, ORIOLES 4 *(First game)*   42 — 14

PITCHER	IP	H	R-ER	BB	SO	ERA
Abbott	2.2	7	3-3	1	0	6.17
Bair (3-0)	3.1	1	0-0	1	3	3.06
Hernandez (S9)	3.0	3	1-1	0	0	2.26

TIGERS 8, ORIOLES 0 *(Second game)*   43 — 14

PITCHER	IP	H	R-ER	BB	SO	ERA
Petry (9-3)	9.0	3	0-0	1	5	2.79

THE showdown concluded with a letdown. We lost two of three games to the Blue Jays, who feathered their nest at the expense of my staff by counting twenty-three runs and thirty-seven hits in the three games.

I am concerned about Jack, who has a mild case of bronchitis and a tender pitching elbow. He has missed only one starting assignment in my five-year association with the Tigers. Now he's going to miss another. There have been other events on the staff: Sid Monge has joined the team. We purchased Sid from the San Diego Padres to give us another left-handed pitcher in the bullpen. I don't know if I can salvage this guy— he needs work.

When we gained one pitcher, we lost another: we had to let Glenn Abbott go to make room for Monge. It's never easy to say good-bye to one of your players, and it's much tougher when that player is a gentleman like Glenn. I talked to him at length and suggested he pursue becoming a minor league pitching coach if he's unable to hook up with another major league club. He doesn't want to return to the minors, which is a natural reaction for someone who has spent ten seasons at the major league level. If he still wants to pitch, he knows that any established pitcher who pitches well enough in the minors will eventually get a call to return to the majors.

This series would have been a total disaster without two and one-third innings of superlative relief from Willie Hernandez in our 5-4 victory on Monday. He's giving the entire league the "willies." The save was his third in the past four games and his tenth of the season—a career-high for Willie.

Sid arrived with a graphic picture of Tiger clout. "I never got such a fast response from my shoe representative. He asked me what kind of trim I needed and said he'd send the shoes Federal Express. If I had gone to Cleveland, it would have been three years before I heard from him."

Monday, June 11
TIGERS 5, BLUE JAYS 4   44 – 14

PITCHER	IP	H	R-ER	BB	SO	ERA
Rozema (2-0)	5.0	4	3-3	0	2	3.06
Monge	0.0	1	0-0	0	0	0.00
Willis	1.2	3	1-1	0	0	2.25
Hernandez (S10)	2.1	1	0-0	0	3	2.17

Tuesday, June 12
BLUE JAYS 12, TIGERS 3   44 – 15

PITCHER	IP	H	R-ER	BB	SO	ERA
Morris (11-3)	3.0	7	6-6	2	3	2.51
Monge	4.0	6	3-2	1	1	4.50
Lopez	1.0	2	3-3	1	0	2.61

Wednesday, June 13
BLUE JAYS 7, TIGERS 3   44 – 16

PITCHER	IP	H	R-ER	BB	SO	ERA
Wilcox (7-4)	5.0	6	4-4	1	2	4.31
Bair	2.0	4	3-3	0	1	3.62
Willis	1.0	1	0-0	0	0	1.80

Y pitching staff is undergoing a facelift. Rookie Carl Willis
has been moved into Morris's spot. Abbott has decided
to accept an optional assignment to our top farm club at Evansville, meaning he's liable to return later this season when
doubleheaders pile up. Rozema has been moved into the starting rotation, even though we can expect no more than six or
seven innings from him.

We have ten games in the next ten days, and without Jack
there isn't a legitimate complete-game pitcher at our disposal.
The bullpen already has twenty-two saves, which is only six
fewer than last season.

Berenguer did give us a complete-game shutout here on
Saturday. This was heartening considering the problems he
has faced.

Monge is my new project. I've worked with Sid in the
bullpen during the past week. The results are encouraging. He
certainly was a mess when he arrived from San Diego. I had
encouraged his purchase simply because we have such an
acute shortage of left-handed pitching in our system. I had not
seen Sid pitch since he was with the Cleveland Indians in 1981,
and reasoned he certainly was better than any left-handed
pitcher we had in the minor leagues. But he'd fallen into a lot
of bad habits. He wasn't getting his hand on top of the ball and
his pitches consequently had no velocity. Some people insist
you can't make a guy throw harder, but you can by correcting
mechanical flaws. We also worked on Sid's split-fingered fastball and he couldn't believe the difference.

I talked to Glenn before he left for Evansville. Glenn is a
control pitcher and he didn't receive enough work to stay sharp.
He was in good spirits when he left, and I feel he'll straighten
himself out to the point that he'll help us in August when we
play four doubleheaders in a span of nine days.

Sid Monge's extra work paid off

Friday, June 15

TIGERS 3, BREWERS 2   45 – 16

PITCHER	IP	H	R-ER	BB	SO	ERA
Petry (10-3)	7.0	7	2-2	0	2	2.78
Hernandez (S11)	2.0	1	0-0	0	2	2.09

Saturday, June 16

TIGERS 6, BREWERS 0   46 – 16

PITCHER	IP	H	R-ER	BB	SO	ERA
Berenguer (4-4)	9.0	5	0-0	3	1	3.00

Sunday, June 17

TIGERS 7, BREWERS 4   47 – 16

PITCHER	IP	H	R-ER	BB	SO	ERA
Rozema (3-0)	5.0	4	1-1	1	0	2.89
Lopez (S8)	4.0	2	3-3	2	2	2.90

THIS is our third straight Monday night nationally televised game of the week. Sometimes they can be a distraction. I know of egocentric managers and coaches who make a point of being seen on national television. This club enjoys prime time. We have players who came to us from all corners of America. Their families do not receive many opportunities to see them perform. National television exposure affords that opportunity.

In addition, this is good training for post-season games. Every game of the league Championship Series and World Series is telecast by a national network. Some players require a little time to be comfortable knowing they're being watched in living rooms from coast to coast. These regular-season telecasts will help prepare players for post-season pressures.

Pressure comes in various forms. Petry, for instance, puts extra pressure on himself with his superstitious habits on days he pitches. Dan gets up in the morning at the same time, eats the same food, sits in a specific spot in the clubhouse, wears the same undershirt, and walks to the bullpen to warm up at the same time. He feels the ritual is successful. I feel this force of habit is too much of a reliance on matters that have no impact on his performance, and invites trouble if the routine is interrupted.

We won two of three games from the New York Yankees, thanks again to our bullpen, which allowed two earned runs in thirteen and two-thirds innings. Hernandez appeared in all three games. He's pitching as well as any relief pitcher I've had or seen, and I had Rollie Fingers. Willie is our most valuable player. He knows he's going to make the All-Star team and he deserves the honor.

Lopez has some mental problems that stem from Willie's emergence as our number one reliever. Aurelio is a high-strung, emotional person who enjoyed being cast as number one bullpen artist. As Willie gradually took over as the king of the bullpen, Aurelio's ego was bruised. I'm going to have to help Aurelio understand his role. Any outstanding relief pitcher needs an advance man to set up save situations. Willie filled that role for Al Holland last year with the Philadelphia Phillies. This year, Aurelio will do that for Willie.

Aurelio preceded Willie in two of the three games in this series. He allowed two runs in one inning in our 7-6 victory on Tuesday. Willie was summoned to retire the final two batters with the tying run on second base. In Wednesday's game, Aurelio allowed the tying run in the eighth inning, but we won, 9-6, in thirteen innings on a three-run home run by Howard Johnson.

Morris threw on the side and is at 95 percent effectiveness. Jack went to see Dr. Robert Teitge, the club's orthopedic specialist. Teitge attempted to drain fluid from Jack's elbow, but there was none present.

Bullpen stalwarts—Doug Bair and Aurelio Lopez

I asked Jim Palmer, a color commentator for ABC-TV and a future Hall of Fame pitcher, to talk with Jack. Jim had coped with elbow injuries throughout his career, and pitched a minimum of 272 innings for eight seasons. That's a lot of pitches. Palmer talked at length with Jack, who was encouraged by the conversation.

Palmer told me he wants to pitch again in the major leagues. I look for Jim to be pitching somewhere in the majors next season. He said he feels good, and indirectly blamed us for his release. He would have been in Baltimore's rotation and received the opportunity to pitch if we had not started so quickly.

I like Palmer, but I like our 49-17 record better.

Monday, June 18
YANKEES 2, TIGERS 1   47 – 17

PITCHER	IP	H	R-ER	BB	SO	ERA
Wilcox (7-5)	7.0	7	2-2	3	7	4.16
Hernandez	2.0	1	0-0	0	0	2.02

Tuesday, June 19
TIGERS 7, YANKEES 6   48 – 17

PITCHER	IP	H	R-ER	BB	SO	ERA
Willis	4.1	9	4-4	0	3	4.82
Bair	2.2	0	0-0	4	1	3.38
Lopez (6-0)	1.1	0	2-0	2	0	2.83
Hernandez (S12)	0.2	0	0-0	0	0	1.99

Wednesday, June 20
TIGERS 9, YANKEES 6 *(13 innings)*   49 – 17

PITCHER	IP	H	R-ER	BB	SO	ERA
Petry	6.0	9	4-4	2	1	2.97
Lopez	1.0	1	1-1	1	0	2.95
Hernandez	4.0	3	1-1	2	4	2.01
Bair (4-0)	2.0	1	0-0	0	2	3.21

J ACK Morris transferred the pain in his elbow to the necks of the Toronto Blue Jays and Baltimore Orioles, who have cricks from looking up at our eight-and-one-half game lead. Jack pitched for the first time in twelve days and had no pain. He allowed one hit in six innings before we lifted him with a 7-0 lead over the Milwaukee Brewers for his one hundredth victory.

We didn't manage a complete game in this series, but received good efforts from Rozema and Wilcox. Rozie was armed with a five-run cushion in the first inning, so I talked with him and Lance about going with sinking fastballs and not becoming too cute. Rozie gave us six innings, with Carl Willis and Willie Hernandez (who else?) finishing. Milt went eight innings in one of his best performances since I joined the Tigers. Bair worked a flawless ninth inning. It seemed strange to come into the clubhouse after the win and not shake Willie's hand.

The only disappointing performance of the weekend came from Juan Berenguer. He didn't have much velocity or location and was defeated by Don Sutton and Rollie Fingers, a pair of old Victrolas who keep on playing.

Thursday, June 21
BREWERS 4, TIGERS 3   49 — 18

PITCHER	IP	H	R-ER	BB	SO	ERA
Berenguer (4-5)	5.1	7	4-4	2	1	3.28
Monge	2.2	1	0-0	1	0	2.70
Lopez	1.0	1	0-0	0	0	2.89

Friday, June 22
TIGERS 7, BREWERS 3   50 — 18

PITCHER	IP	H	R-ER	BB	SO	ERA
Rozema (4-0)	6.0	5	3-3	1	1	3.12
Willis	0.2	0	0-0	1	0	4.50
Hernandez (S13)	2.1	1	0-0	1	5	1.94

Saturday, June 23
TIGERS 5, BREWERS 1   51 — 18

PITCHER	IP	H	R-ER	BB	SO	ERA
Wilcox (8-5)	8.0	4	1-1	2	4	3.90
Bair	1.0	0	0-0	0	1	3.14

Sunday, June 24
TIGERS 7, BREWERS 1   52 — 18

PITCHER	IP	H	R-ER	BB	SO	ERA
Morris (12-3)	6.0	1	0-0	0	4	2.39
Lopez (S9)	3.0	2	1-1	0	0	2.90

Y ANKEE Stadium is a beautiful ballpark since it was remod-
eled in 1974-75, and is a treasure chest of personal memories. I was in four World Series as a player—three with the
Dodgers and one with the St. Louis Cardinals—and the
Yankees were the opposition three times.

We lost two of three games to the Yankees and still gained
one and one-half games in the standings on the Toronto Blue
Jays. This is an omen. Yankee Stadium is the last ballpark we'll
play in during the regular season, with four games here in late
September. I have a strong suspicion we'll be plotting strategy
for the American League Championship Series.

Our play here was not of championship caliber, although
we did take some precautions for Hernandez, which probably
cost us a victory in the final game. Willie had appeared in six
of our previous nine games and needed a day off. We never
allowed Willie to leave the dugout as the Yankees scored three
runs in the eighth inning off Carl Willis to erase our 4-2 lead.
Willie leads the league in appearances (thirty-five) and has
pitched two or more innings twenty times. He is a little tired,
even though he's too proud to admit fatigue.

The two games we lost here marked the first time this
season our bullpen has met defeat by relinquishing leads in
the late innings. Dave Winfield inflicted the first loss by smack-
ing Doug Bair's one and only pitch off the left-center-field wall.
I seem to bring out the best in Winfield, who played for me at
San Diego. He's hitting .684 (13-19) against us this season.
We better rewrite our book on Winfield, which presently has
instructions to jam him with low fastballs.

Most upsetting in this series was Berenguer's pitching in
the second game. We armed Juan with a 4-0 lead after two
innings, but were forced to remove him in the third when he
surrendered two runs and departed with the tying run on base.
Juan was dejected. He reluctantly handed Sparky the ball and
trudged to the dugout. This is proper decorum for a pitcher

Willie received some rest, and it cost us a game

who is removed from a game. There is a standing rule that no pitcher will show up Sparky in this situation. We do not want our pitchers to express disgust. This is an embarrassment to the pitcher and Sparky, and results in a substantial fine levied against the pitcher. Sparky simply asks the pitcher to hand him the ball. The pitcher had better comply. Some pitchers disagree, although not vehemently. Others hand you the ball and virtually beg for removal. Fortunately, we don't have any quitters on our club. We want pitchers who aren't happy to leave the game. I'd rather have a pitcher come in and kick the water cooler than someone who is resigned to failure.

Lance Parrish frequently has to serve as pitching coach or manager, especially when we have used one of our two allotted visits to the mound and don't want to remove the pitcher. A lot of work has gone into polishing Lance as a capable catcher. He was too aloof in his formative years and had to learn to take charge. This is his staff, too. He must instill confidence in the pitchers and offer in-game observations that can help guide a pitcher to a successful performance.

Monday, June 25
YANKEES 7, TIGERS 3   52 – 19

PITCHER	IP	H	R-ER	BB	SO	ERA
Petry	6.1	11	3-3	2	2	3.05
Bair (4-1)	0.0	1	1-0	0	0	3.14
Hernandez	1.0	2	3-3	3	1	2.32
Willis	0.2	0	0-0	0	0	4.22

Tuesday, June 26
TIGERS 9, YANKEES 7 *(10 innings)*   53 – 19

PITCHER	IP	H	R-ER	BB	SO	ERA
Berenguer	2.1	5	3-3	1	0	3.54
Lopez	3.2	4	3-3	2	5	3.16
Monge	1.1	2	1-1	0	2	3.38
Hernandez (3-0)	2.2	1	0-0	0	2	2.23

Wednesday, June 27
YANKEES 5, TIGERS 4   53 – 20

PITCHER	IP	H	R-ER	BB	SO	ERA
Rozema	6.0	5	2-2	2	0	3.10
Willis (0-1)	1.0	2	3-3	1	0	6.17
Bair	1.0	0	0-0	1	0	3.07

O UR success has brought a lot of fan mail. Most of the letters I receive involve the split-fingered fastball. One came from a ten-year-old youngster named Kyle, from Lockport, N.Y.

> I pitch and play second base in a midget league. I have heard on television that you have taught most of the pitchers for Detroit how to throw a split-fingered fastball. Could you please tell me how to throw it? Thank you very much.
> P.S. If you cannot write back, next time on national television you could show me how to do this. This September when you play the Blue Jays in Toronto I'll be there. Maybe you could come to my house afterwards.

I'm going to make a point to call Kyle and invite him to a game in Toronto as my guest. I'll talk to him after the game and maybe even show him the proper way to throw the split-fingered fastball.

Right now, I have to concentrate on my staff. There are warning signals. Morris allowed ten hits and five runs in five innings in a loss to the Minnesota Twins. Wilcox also permitted five runs in five innings, but we received a lift from Lopez and Hernandez, who pitched a combined four innings of shutout relief in a 7-5 victory. Berenguer, who needs a good outing more than any other starting pitcher, was disappointing again. Juan was tagged for six runs in five innings in a 9-0 defeat. He hasn't pitched well since he was struck in the head by Al Bumbry's line drive in Baltimore.

The one starter who fared well in this series was Petry. He matched his career-high strikeouts with ten and beat the Twins, 4-3, with support from Willie. Dan is becoming more aggressive with each outing. Dan is 11-3 and there is talk of him being selected for the All-Star game, just around the corner. The numbers might get him, though. Jack and Willie seem certain to be chosen by Joe Altobelli of the Baltimore Orioles and three pitchers from one team is very unusual.

Friday, June 29

TWINS 5, TIGERS 3 *(First game)*   53 – 21

PITCHER	IP	H	R-ER	BB	SO	ERA
Morris (12-4)	5.2	10	5-5	3	2	2.63
Bair	3.1	2	0-0	1	0	2.85

TIGERS 7, TWINS 5 *(Second game)*   54 – 21

PITCHER	IP	H	R-ER	BB	SO	ERA
Wilcox	5.0	5	5-5	1	4	4.16
Lopez	2.1	2	0-0	2	0	3.05
Hernandez (4-0)	1.2	1	0-0	0	1	2.18

Saturday, June 30

TIGERS 4, TWINS 3   55 – 21

PITCHER	IP	H	R-ER	BB	SO	ERA
Petry (11-3)	8.1	7	3-3	3	10	3.06
Hernandez (S14)	0.2	0	0-0	0	1	2.15

Sunday, July 1

TWINS 9, TIGERS 0   55 – 22

PITCHER	IP	H	R-ER	BB	SO	ERA
Berenguer (4-6)	5.0	7	6-5	1	2	3.89
Willis	2.0	3	1-1	1	1	5.93
Monge	2.0	1	2-0	1	1	2.70

Pitching coaches have feelings, too. I'm upset for two reasons. Foremost is our starting pitching. We haven't had a
complete game since June 16, and my staff was bludgeoned
for twenty-four runs and twenty-eight hits in losing three straight
games to the Chicago White Sox. We still have a seven-game
lead on the Blue Jays, but we're not playing very well. Pitching
has been our key the entire season and, except for the bullpen,
our pitching has gone into hibernation. We're 20-20 after our
35-5 start. We've lost four consecutive games for the first time,
seven of ten, and seem to have forgotten our killer instinct.
Every club I've ever been associated with has experienced
pitching slumps. You just have to battle your way out. Even
Sparky is depressed.

I'm also upset because rookie reliever Carl Willis was optioned to Evansville to make room for shortstop Doug Baker.
Alan Trammell has some tendinitis in his right shoulder and
needs a rest. I guess the Tigers knew how much I liked Willis
because I wasn't consulted before this move was made. Sometimes clubs have to make decisions on the spur of the moment. I like to believe I was unavailable when general manager
Bill Lajoie and Sparky came to this decision. This had never
before happened to me in my five-year association with the
Tigers. I called Carl. At least he was in a good frame of mind.

Monday, July 2
WHITE SOX 7, TIGERS 1   55 – 23

PITCHER	IP	H	R-ER	BB	SO	ERA
Rozema (4-1)	4.0	5	4-4	2	2	3.54
Lopez	2.0	2	3-0	1	1	2.91
Monge	2.0	1	0-0	2	0	2.25

Tuesday, July 3
WHITE SOX 9, TIGERS 5   55 – 24

PITCHER	IP	H	R-ER	BB	SO	ERA
Morris (12-5)	4.1	9	8-8	2	1	3.08
Bair	2.2	1	0-0	0	2	2.70
Hernandez	1.0	1	1-1	0	1	2.25

Sparky's the boss, so Carl Willis got his pink slip

Wednesday, July 4

WHITE SOX 8, TIGERS 2   55 – 25

PITCHER	IP	H	R-ER	BB	SO	ERA
Wilcox (8-6)	5.2	5	6-6	7	2	4.46
Lopez	0.1	1	0-0	1	0	2.94
Monge	2.0	2	2-2	1	1	3.21

MORRIS has created a lot of flak the past couple of days. Jack seemed a shoo-in for the All-Star team until reports from the league office began to circulate that no starting pitcher used on Sunday would be selected to participate in the All-Star game on Tuesday. Jack had been scheduled for a Sunday assignment. And Jack was incensed when he made the team because Petry was not selected. Dan was disappointed and reticent. I guess there's a time and place for everything.

Kirk Gibson picked the right time and place by hitting a three-run home run in the ninth inning to culminate a six-run rally with two outs and propel us to a 7-4 conquest of the Texas Rangers. Our unbelievable comeback ended the four-game losing skid and left me limp. This was probably the most excited I've been all season. As a coach, you try to exercise patience. You implore the players to exercise that quality until the slump is over, but, believe me, it's tough to sit back and wait for an explosion such as the one provided by Gibson.

The bullpen was also heroic. Bair, Lopez, and Hernandez provided us with three and one-third scoreless innings in relief of Petry. I talked to Dan about his absence from the All-Star squad. Joe Altobelli, the American League manager for the game, was trapped in a no-win situation. He was bound to ruffle someone's feathers but couldn't justify choosing three pitchers from the same team. Dan was more hurt than upset. The first thing he said to me was "I'll make it next year."

TIGERS 7, RANGERS 4   56 – 25

PITCHER	IP	H	R-ER	BB	SO	ERA
Petry	5.2	8	4-4	2	5	3.22
Bair	1.1	0	0-0	1	0	2.63
Lopez (7-0)	1.2	1	0-0	0	0	2.87
Hernandez (S15)	0.1	0	0-0	0	1	2.24

I'M at my wit's end with Berenguer. I've tried everything in my power to get Juan straightened out. Now I'm back to square one. Juan didn't get out of the third inning in a 5-3 loss to the Texas Rangers. He continues to work hard, but he isn't pitching with much confidence. That is a mystery to me because he gets the ball as frequently as any starting pitcher.

Morris gave me a figurative belt to the stomach by insisting he wanted to resume throwing his changeup. Jack has experienced a couple of sub-par outings and feels that opposing hitters are laying off his split-fingered fastball and sitting on his fastball. Jack threw the changeup until late in the 1982 season. The pitch was effective at times, but I encouraged him to dump it in favor of the split-fingered fastball because I believed the changeup reduced the efficiency of his fastball. I acceded to Jack's wishes, but advised him to throw the change-up only if his split-fingered fastball wasn't working properly. After all, I reminded him, the split-finger was the reason he progressed from being a good pitcher to becoming an outstanding pitcher.

My staff certainly is testing me.

RANGERS 5, TIGERS 3   56 — 26

PITCHER	IP	H	R-ER	BB	SO	ERA
Berenguer (4-7)	2.2	5	3-3	2	2	4.09
Monge	1.0	2	0-0	0	1	3.00
Lopez	4.1	5	2-2	1	4	2.95

M ORRIS is mad. Sometimes I think Jack was born in a hornet's nest. We advised him that he will not start on Sunday. He has had a stiff neck and is recovering from tendinitis in his right elbow. Complete rest, we believe, is the best therapy. We want to be certain that Jack's arm is completely sound for the second half of the season. This decision really weighed heavily on Sparky's mind. He felt Jack wouldn't make the All-Star team if he pitched Sunday. The consequences, Sparky believed, would be a Jack Morris with a poor attitude. Jack has a lot of pride and hates to miss a start. But, we're going to need lots of innings from Jack and Petry or else our bullpen will be led to slaughter.

We went to that bullpen again tonight after Rozema kept us in the game for his customary six innings. Dave was removed with a 4-2 lead. Sparky went to Hernandez, who permitted just one hit in three innings in our 5-2 victory.

Willie actually spends very little time in the bullpen. He stays in the clubhouse a lot, which I don't really like. Willie will watch television to study opposing hitters, and he's accused of taking naps during the early innings of games when he knows he won't be used. The players kid Willie a lot about sleeping. He usually appears in the dugout around the sixth inning. If I nod to him he heads for the bullpen. If I raise my left hand he heads to the bullpen and starts throwing. My left hand is having a field day.

TIGERS 5, RANGERS 2   57 – 26

PITCHER	IP	H	R-ER	BB	SO	ERA
Rozema (5-1)	6.0	9	2-2	1	3	3.49
Hernandez (S16)	3.0	1	0-0	3	5	2.15

OUR All-Star break numbers are imposing: 57-27 record, a seven-game lead over the Toronto Blue Jays, and six players—Jack Morris, Willie Hernandez, Lou Whitaker, Chet Lemon, Alan Trammell, and Lance Parrish—on the All-Star team. But in spite of the numbers, we've got problems.

Trammell, our Gold Glove shortstop, was removed from tonight's game with numbness in two fingers of his right hand. He probably will miss his All-Star date, and faces the distinct possibility of being placed on the disabled list.

Closer to my heart, our starting pitchers are faltering. Bair was hit hard tonight in a 9-7 loss. Over our past forty-four games (22-22) the composite earned run average of our starters is 5.30 and they have averaged just five and one-third innings per start. We've managed to stay afloat because of the bullpen, whose earned run average over the corresponding forty-four games is 2.96. Willie has appeared in twenty-one of the past forty-four games and has an ERA of 1.36.

We need this break. The season is only going to get tougher. At this time, I'm leaning toward retirement at the close of this season.

RANGERS 9, TIGERS 7   57 – 27

PITCHER	IP	H	R-ER	BB	SO	ERA
Bair (4-2)	2.2	9	6-6	0	0	3.50
Berenguer	3.1	5	2-2	0	1	4.15
Lopez	2.0	2	1-1	1	1	2.99

FIRST-HALF STATISTICS

STARTERS	Won	Lost	IP	ERA	GS	
Abbott	1	1	11.1	9.53	3	
Bair	0	1	2.2	20.22	1	
Berenguer	4	7	80.1	4.09	15	
Morris	12	5	134.1	3.08	18	
Petry	11	3	120.1	3.22	19	
Rozema	5	1	46.1	4.27	9	
Wilcox	8	6	103.0	4.46	18	
Willis	0	0	4.1	8.31	1	
Totals	41	24	502.2	4.39	84	

RELIEVERS	Won	Lost	IP	ERA	G	Saves
Abbott	1	1	12.0	3.00	5	0
Bair	4	1	51.1	2.63	24	3
Berenguer	0	0	3.1	5.41	1	0
Hernandez	4	0	75.1	2.15	40	16
Lopez	7	0	75.1	2.99	37	9
Monge	0	0	15.0	3.00	8	0
Rozema	0	0	13.0	0.69	6	0
Willis	0	1	9.1	4.82	7	0
Totals	16	3	254.2	2.65	128	28

Our worst fears have been realized. Trammell has been placed on the disabled list with tendinitis in his right shoulder and a problem with his ulnar nerve. In spite of this setback, we won three of four games from the Minnesota Twins on the Metrodome's rug, while allowing only ten earned runs and issuing four walks in forty-one innings.

Petry lost a tough game in the opener, 4-2, thanks in part to a poor execution of fundamentals by our defense. The coaching staff retired to Sparky's suite at the Hyatt Hotel following the game to analyze our situation. The meeting focused on preventing a letdown. We emphasized intensity and a dedication to working a little harder with the players on fundamentals. Sparky held a team meeting the next day and asked the players to perform with more intensity. He urged them to play hard each day and not dwell on our record or our lead. Sparky said he had no secret recipe for winning. He did, however, assure each player personal satisfaction if they simply gave as much of themselves as possible. The players responded by winning the next three games, two of which were extra-inning affairs.

Hernandez and Lopez allowed two hits in three and two-thirds innings on Friday and we won, 5-3, in eleven innings. Bair and Willie permitted one hit in six and one-third innings of our 6-5 triumph in twelve innings on Saturday, and Lopey surrendered only one hit in three and two-thirds innings to preserve Rozema's 6-2 victory on Sunday. Talk about relief! Our bullpen should do a commercial for Rolaids.

Our record is 60-28. The bullpen has figured in forty-eight of those victories with thirty saves and eighteen wins. Willie, Aurelio, and Doug are 17-1 with all thirty saves. We're figuring on a hundred victories to win our division, and we're counting on fifty saves to guarantee those hundred victories. Only four American League teams have reached fifty saves in one season. Those four are the 1970 Twins (fifty-eight), the 1965 Chicago White Sox (fifty-three), the 1966 Baltimore Orioles (fifty-one), and the 1980 New York Yankees (fifty). We'll make five.

Berenguer has been replaced in the starting rotation by Glenn Abbott. He still is not pitching effectively, but Glenn has pitched well at Evansville.

Thursday, July 12
TWINS 4, TIGERS 2   57 – 28

PITCHER	IP	H	R-ER	BB	SO	ERA
Petry (11-4)	7.1	9	4-3	0	2	3.24
Bair	0.2	0	0-0	0	1	3.46

Friday, July 13
TIGERS 5, TWINS 3 *(11 innings)*   58 – 28

PITCHER	IP	H	R-ER	BB	SO	ERA
Morris	7.1	8	3-1	0	3	2.99
Hernandez (5-0)	2.2	1	0-0	2	1	2.08
Lopez (S10)	1.0	1	0-0	1	0	2.95

Saturday, July 14
TIGERS 6, TWINS 5 *(12 innings)*   59 – 28

PITCHER	IP	H	R-ER	BB	SO	ERA
Wilcox	5.2	8	4-4	0	2	4.56
Bair	3.1	0	0-0	0	2	3.26
Hernandez (6-0)	3.0	1	1-1	0	1	2.11

Sunday, July 15
TIGERS 6, TWINS 2   60 – 28

PITCHER	IP	H	R-ER	BB	SO	ERA
Rozema (6-1)	5.1	8	2-1	1	5	3.20
Lopez (S11)	3.2	1	0-0	0	5	2.81

GLENN Abbott pitched our first complete game since June 16 in defeating the Chicago White Sox 7-1. No one expected Glenn to go the distance, but this guy isn't an excitable rookie. Glenn played for the World Champion Oakland A's in 1974 and combined with Vida Blue, Paul Lindblad, and Rollie Fingers for a no-hit game against the California Angels on September 28, 1975. Glenn is the type of pitcher I appreciate. He doesn't have the greatest stuff in the world, but is a student of pitching. His powers of concentration and observation have kept him at the major league level.

I think Bill Lajoie, our general manager, deserves a lot of credit for his handling of Glenn. Bill was candid with him when Glenn was assigned to Evansville. There were no guarantees of a return trip to Detroit, but Bill recognized our need for pitching and gave Glenn some hope. Bill even footed Glenn's hotel bill at Evansville as a show of good faith, and then made a point of seeing him pitch. Bill detected that Glenn had gotten away from throwing the tight slider he used last season when he fashioned a 1.93 earned run average. A pitching coach can't be too proud.

During the game we became involved in a verbal spat with the White Sox over brushback pitches. Glenn threw inside on Scott Fletcher and in the sixth inning hit Carlton Fisk. Chicago manager Tony LaRussa retaliated in the eighth inning by instructing Britt Burns to hit Lance Parrish. LaRussa maintained that Glenn had hit Fisk on purpose. That's utterly preposterous because we enjoyed a 5-0 lead and the hit batsman brought up Harold Baines with two runners on base. Basically, I like LaRussa. He's just too brash at times. Lance, though, has no affection for LaRussa, calling him "Mr. Tough Guy." I enjoyed the exchange. Lance hasn't had a base hit in his past ten at-bats, and has been mired in a prolonged slump. I think he requires an emotional boost now and then. LaRussa has provided that boost.

I'm glad these three—Gibson, Trammell, Parrish—are Tigers

TIGERS 7, WHITE SOX 1   61 — 28

PITCHER	IP	H	R-ER	BB	SO	ERA
Abbott (3-2)	9.0	5	1-1	1	0	4.73

DAN Petry worked seven and two-thirds innings, received relief from Hernandez, and improved his record to 12-4 with a 3-2 victory over the Chicago White Sox. Dan finally believes he can be a number one pitcher. I've always told him that once he believes in his abilities as much as I do he will emerge as a dominant pitcher.

There are a few reasons for the budding of Petry. One is the emphasis on his fastball. Another is the use of a straight changeup to replace his split-fingered fastball as an off-speed pitch. Dan feels more comfortable throwing the changeup, and I don't object as long as he's successful. This has translated into fewer bases on balls, eleven in his past sixty-one innings, and fewer home runs, eight for the season after having the dubious distinction of leading the major leagues last season with thirty-seven. I also can measure Petry's growth by his post-game comments. He told reporters he had approached this game as a vendetta against the White Sox because he didn't appreciate what happened to Lance Parrish the previous night.

Incidentally, Lance collected two hits and scored a run.

TIGERS 3, WHITE SOX 2   62 – 28

PITCHER	IP	H	R-ER	BB	SO	ERA
Petry (12-4)	7.2	5	2-2	1	5	3.19
Hernandez (S17)	1.1	0	0-0	0	3	2.08

WEDNESDAY, JULY 18   DETROIT

O UR five-game winning streak died in a Morris tantrum. He
flew into a fit over a borderline ball-strike call by home
plate umpire Mark Johnson and proceeded to lose 3-1 and
4-3 leads in a 10-6 loss to the White Sox.

Jack seems unable to comprehend the serious nature of
his frustrations. He ranted and raved. He embarrassed me, himself, Sparky, and the front office. He incensed his teammates.
Quite obviously, Jack has a lot of growing up to do. He's not
having fun pitching and he's not a happy person.

I did not talk to Jack following the game, but he's going
to hear from me tomorrow.

WHITE SOX 10, TIGERS 6   62 – 29

PITCHER	IP	H	R-ER	BB	SO	ERA
Morris (12-6)	4.0	10	7-7	2	1	3.34
Bair	1.0	1	0-0	1	0	3.20
Monge	1.0	1	0-0	0	1	2.81
Berenguer	1.1	2	2-2	2	1	4.29
Lopez	1.2	2	1-1	0	0	2.87

I hope I salvaged a man's pride and self-esteem today in my lengthy pre-game talk with Morris. We transcended baseball and discussed life. The talk was very emotional for both of us. Jack unabashedly shed some tears. I expressed some very human feelings because I love this guy. There was a large dose of mutual respect.

I told Jack that money isn't the key to happiness. Happiness stems from battling your hardest every night and then walking into the clubhouse to face your teammates, coaches, and manager, knowing you did your best. That feeling earns respect. I told him he didn't have respect last night because he didn't battle.

There's a certain amount of ambivalence in Jack's makeup. He has tremendous pride and feels he lets the team down if he doesn't win, but becomes so upset that he blames other circumstances and other people for his failings. Jack is a melancholy guy even when everything falls into place for him. He simply hasn't learned to channel adversity. He self-destructs. Great pitchers demonstrate composure, pride, and competitive instincts. They don't allow trivial things to upset them. They know the other dugout realizes that if a game is close the emotional pitcher will beat himself. That's exactly what happened last night—Jack beat himself. Now he has retreated into a shell; he says he'll no longer discuss baseball with the media.

I don't want to hurt Jack. I want to help him. That's another side of my job as pitching coach. I drew on some advice offered to me by the late Fresco Thompson in 1968, my first year as manager of the Los Angeles Dodgers' minor league affiliate at Albuquerque. Fresco told me never to take anything for granted. At times, I have taken Jack for granted. I expected greatness from him every time he took the mound, and I didn't feel he needed special attention. But right now, Jack needs my attention more than anyone. The players are upset, and have accused Jack of pouting. He is becoming an alien in his own clubhouse.

Wilcox turned in one of his finest efforts of the season in defeating the Texas Rangers 9-2. Milt allowed two runs in seven and one-third innings and didn't walk anyone. He has had three injections of cortisone in his pitching shoulder since the season began. This is an inordinate amount of medication, but he feels the shots are beneficial. Mental attitude is important to the psychology of pitching.

TIGERS 9, RANGERS 2   63 — 29

PITCHER	IP	H	R-ER	BB	SO	ERA
Wilcox (9-6)	7.1	8	2-2	0	7	4.42
Hernandez	0.2	1	0-0	0	1	2.06
Lopez	1.0	1	0-0	0	1	2.83

TIGER Stadium is Dave Rozema's Magic Kingdom. How else do you explain the fact that Dave has won fifteen consecutive decisions at Tiger Stadium since 1980?

Dave's performance tonight was vintage Rozema—ninety-five pitches and no walks in eight innings. We slipped past the Texas Rangers 3-1, with ninth-inning relief from Mr. Hernandez.

Our record is 64-29. We're the first Tiger team to be thirty-five games over .500 since the 1968 World Champions. The Blue Jays are eight games out and the Orioles are trailing by thirteen. We're playing well and I feel that corresponds to our pitching, which has posted a 2.58 earned run average with just eleven walks (three intentional) in winning seven of nine games. Our little slump is over.

TIGERS 3, RANGERS 1   64 – 29

PITCHER	IP	H	R-ER	BB	SO	ERA
Rozema (7-1)	8.0	6	1-1	0	4	2.97
Hernandez (S18)	1.0	0	0-0	0	1	2.04

SATURDAY, JULY 21   DETROIT

T HE hours I spent in the bullpen correcting Sid Monge's flaws paid off tonight. Sid permitted one unearned run in four innings to earn a 7-6 victory over the Rangers. I'm not after feathers in my cap, but Sid needed a lot of work when he joined us. Sid deserves a lot of credit for his perseverance.

Bair and Hernandez tacked on two and two-thirds innings of scoreless relief to drop our bullpen's earned run average to 1.20 in thirty innings since the All-Star break.

We continue to search for solid pitching from our second-line starters. Abbott was hit hard tonight and didn't get beyond the third inning. Glenn is not a power pitcher and has below-average stuff but he is above average in terms of control and composure. He did not have his control tonight.

TIGERS 7, RANGERS 6   65 – 29

PITCHER	IP	H	R-ER	BB	SO	ERA
Abbott	2.1	5	5-4	0	0	5.45
Monge (1-0)	4.0	3	1-0	0	4	2.25
Bair	0.2	0	0-0	0	0	3.17
Hernandez (S19)	2.0	1	0-0	0	1	1.99

Tiger Stadium has been a Magic Kingdom for Dave Rozema

SUNDAY, JULY 22   DETROIT

TODAY I watched Petry and Hernandez master the Texas Rangers, 2-0, on four singles, to complete a four-game sweep. Dan, our Cy Young candidate, pitched eight and two-thirds innings to improve his record to 13-4. Willie, our MVP candidate, retired Pete O'Brien for the final out and has four wins and seven saves in his past thirteen appearances.

I can't say enough about either one of these fellows. Willie is like Janitor in a Drum the way he cleans up on opposing hitters. Dan's earned run average hasn't been higher than 3.24 all season, and now rests comfortably at 3.00. He has made himself the equal of Morris, which contributes to some keen competition. Dan was asked by reporters about a possible Cy Young award. He dismissed that talk as premature, but added that his fondest wish was to tie Jack for the league lead in victories.

There are certain qualities that are tough to teach. One is a person's general overview of himself. "My dad always told me I don't have to tell anybody how good I am, and that's fresh in my memory," Dan said after the game. "All that matters is what I do on the field."

TIGERS 2, RANGERS 0   66 – 29

PITCHER	IP	H	R-ER	BB	SO	ERA
Petry (13-4)	8.2	4	0-0	1	8	3.00
Hernandez (S20)	0.1	0	0-0	0	0	1.98

I am now the voice of Jack Morris, which puts me in a rather awkward position. Reporters pepper me with questions now that Jack refuses to talk. I'm trying to cooperate with them, but there are some things Jack told me in strictest confidence and I simply can't betray that confidence.

I heaped praise on Jack here on Monday. He battled the Cleveland Indians on a hot, muggy night that adversely affected the control of his split-fingered fastball. Jack walked five batters in six innings and went to the resin bag often in an attempt to keep his pitching hand free of sweat. He gave us six shutout innings in our 4-1 victory. This was Jack's first victory since June 24 and demonstrated that our conversation of the previous week was fruitful. I had asked Jack to maintain his composure, which he did.

We split the final two games, with Wilcox winning on Tuesday and Rozema losing on Wednesday despite a strong performance. We now have an 11-3 record without Trammell. Alan is one of our best—if not *the* best—offensive players. Remember, too, that we won seven of ten games in Jack's absence late in June. That's an 18-6 record without Jack and Alan.

Monday, July 23
TIGERS 4, INDIANS 1 67 – 29

PITCHER	IP	H	R-ER	BB	SO	ERA
Morris (13-6)	6.0	5	0-0	5	5	3.20
Lopez	1.1	0	0-0	4	0	2.79
Bair	1.2	1	1-1	0	1	3.23

Tuesday, July 24
TIGERS 9, INDIANS 5   68 – 29

PITCHER	IP	H	R-ER	BB	SO	ERA
Wilcox (10-6)	6.2	5	4-0	1	4	4.18
Hernandez	2.1	2	1-1	0	2	2.03

Wednesday, July 25
INDIANS 4, TIGERS 1   68 – 30

PITCHER	IP	H	R-ER	BB	SO	ERA
Rozema (7-2)	6.1	7	4-3	0	4	3.08
Lopez	1.2	0	0-0	2	1	2.73

Win number eleven was special for Wilcox

THE Boston Red Sox marched in here with six consecutive victories and nine in ten games. Boston was a team on the move, looking ahead to second place and forcing the Blue Jays and Orioles to watch out below. I must confess that we were a bit fearful of Boston's version of a murderer's row— Dwight Evans, Jim Rice, Tony Armas, and Mike Easler. They arrived for this series with a combined total of eighty-three home runs and 268 RBIs at the two-thirds mark of the season.

We did a pitching number on the entire Red Sox team, splitting the four-game series and allowing only eight runs and three extra-base hits.

Now we play thirteen games, including four doubleheaders, in the next nine days. Pitching generally faces its acid test during this, the hottest portion of the season. We have remained in a five-man rotation for nearly six weeks to provide

our starting pitchers with as much physical and mental rest as possible. The plan is working. Since the All-Star break, we've won thirteen of eighteen games and our staff has an earned run average of 2.29. Four of our five losses came in games in which the opposition had scored four or fewer runs. There is, in fact, a distinct pattern developing that demonstrates the impact pitching has had on our success. Our team earned run average was 2.58 in running off thirty-five victories in our first forty games. It soared to 4.41 in splitting the next forty-four games, and has dipped to 2.29 in winning thirteen of eighteen starts since the All-Star break.

Petry and Wilcox secured our victories against the Red Sox. Dan's 9-1 triumph in the series opener pushed him to the top of the league's victory list with fourteen. Milt pitched eight innings to combine with Hernandez for a 3-0 shutout in the series finale. Milt had Boston chasing breaking pitches in the dirt because he consistently was ahead in the count. There was a great amount of personal satisfaction attached to this victory, which was Milt's eleventh of the season. That figure matches his total for the entire 1983 campaign.

Jack lost his start, 3-2, but pitched good enough to win. He lost in the eighth inning on an error and a couple of tainted hits. Jack was entitled to be upset. Instead, he maintained his composure.

Friday, July 27
TIGERS 9, RED SOX 1 *(First game)*   69 – 30

PITCHER	IP	H	R-ER	BB	SO	ERA
Petry (14-4)	9.0	6	1-1	3	4	2.88

RED SOX 4, TIGERS 0 *(Second game)*   69 – 31

PITCHER	IP	H	R-ER	BB	SO	ERA
Abbott (3-3)	3.1	10	4-4	1	1	5.92
Berenguer	2.2	3	0-0	0	3	4.16
Monge	1.0	0	0-0	0	0	2.14
Bair	1.0	2	0-0	0	1	3.18
Lopez	1.0	0	0-0	0	1	2.70

Saturday, July 28
RED SOX 3, TIGERS 2   69 – 32

PITCHER	IP	H	R-ER	BB	SO	ERA
Morris (13-7)	7.0	8	3-2	3	7	3.18
Hernandez	2.0	0	0-0	1	2	1.99

Sunday, July 29
TIGERS 3, RED SOX 0   70 – 32

PITCHER	IP	H	R-ER	BB	SO	ERA
Wilcox (11-6)	8.0	3	0-0	0	4	3.93
Hernandez (S21)	1.0	0	0-0	0	0	1.96

I have reached the bottom of the ninth inning in a game that lasted thirty-five years. I have decided to retire at the end of this season. Baseball has been the ride of my life. No one really knows with absolute certainty when the trip is over, but during the All-Star break I realized that thirty-five years of buses, planes, and trains is enough for any man. Money is no object. I'm one of the highest-paid pitching coaches. Pride and ego are not considerations. I've given the Tigers about as much as I have to offer in terms of teaching and helping the organization. I'm sure that when spring training rolls around next February baseball will tug at my heart. But I view my retirement as the first day on a new job.

At the age of fifty-four, the time has come for me to devote attention to my wife, Carolyn, and our four children, and to help raise our three grandchildren. We have forty acres in Southern California, whose only occupants right now are trees and a stream. The Craigs have grand designs of adding a log cabin, a well, a barn, and a spirit of living as partners with nature. I'll be splitting rails, instead of teaching split-fingered fastballs.

The toughest part of my decision was informing Sparky, who brought me to Detroit at the beginning of the 1980 season. I have never been associated with anyone more dedicated to baseball than Sparky, and I've rubbed shoulders with many of the game's most storied names. Sparky is Mr. Baseball because he gives so much of himself. His presence in Detroit is a great asset for the Tigers, the city, and the state. My decision did not surprise Sparky. He knows me like a book and he understands my reasoning. Sparky did not resist my decision and that helped ease the pain. I didn't want to hurt him after we've worked so hard as a team for five years to build a championship club.

I've been proud of my years with the Tigers, a first-class organization. My decision is final and I will not entertain offers from any other organization.

Three loves in my life—daughters Sherri, Teresa, and Vikki

GUILLERMO Villanueva Hernandez was born in Aguaya, Puerto Rico, the seventh of nine children. His parents, Dioncio and Dominga, raised their children on a steady diet of baseball. Willie, like many Puerto Rican youngsters, taped his worn-out baseball and nailed together broken bats. Willie blossomed into an amateur first baseman/outfielder of some stature, but never pitched until one month prior to being signed to a Philadelphia Phillies contract by former major league infielder Ruben Amaro. He was pressed into pitching duties because his amateur team's staff was overworked.

Willie languished in the majors as a rather mediocre middle reliever until 1983 when his catcher at Philadelphia, Bo Diaz, encouraged him to use the screwball he had learned from Mike Cuellar. Willie has put that screwball to good use this season. He notched his twenty-second save in preserving a 2-1 victory for Jack Morris, allowing us to split a four-game series with the Cleveland Indians. The twenty-two saves are the most for a Tiger since John Hiller recorded thirty-eight in 1973. The appearance was Willie's thirty-second in which he has entered with a lead. He has not relinquished any of those leads, which is one reason why he was named the league's pitcher of the month for July.

We now embark on our most taxing period of the season—a ten-day stretch in which we play twelve games, including three doubleheaders on consecutive days. We're fortunate to have a bullpen that thrives on work. Willie's arm is so attuned to daily work that he complained of fatigue after working one and two-thirds innings in the third game of the Indians series, a 6-2 loss sustained by Petry. Willie worked on two days' rest and said he felt as if he'd pitched nine innings. Two days without work are too many for Willie.

There isn't much a pitching coach can do to adequately prepare his staff for three consecutive doubleheaders, but our phenomenal bullpen makes me look like a genius. Our staff allowed just nine earned runs in this four-game series. The bullpen trio of Doug, Willie, and Aurelio surrendered one run in twelve innings. Juan pitched well for the first time in a long time in winning the series opener. Dan pitched well in defeat. He just can't solve Cleveland outfielder George Vukovich, who hit a pair of home runs and has four in his last fourteen at-bats against him. Jack didn't pitch exceptionally well in winning his fourteenth game. I wish Jack would talk to the press; as it now stands, I have to answer for him, and my answers may not be what he wants to read.

I visited club president Jim Campbell in his third-floor office and informed him of my decision to retire. Jim is the best club executive I've known. I always have been able to talk comfortably with him about any decisions or on any subject. I have the utmost respect for Jim. He regretted hearing my decision and hoped I would change my mind, and then expressed a desire to retain my services as a scout in the Southern California area. During the course of our conversation, Jim received a call from John E. Fetzer, who owned the Tigers for several years before selling last October to Tom Monaghan. Mr. Fetzer complimented me on the job I have done for the Tigers, and asked me to reconsider my retirement. I respectfully declined.

Tuesday, July 31

TIGERS 5, INDIANS 1 *(First game)*   71 – 32

PITCHER	IP	H	R-ER	BB	SO	ERA
Berenguer (5-7)	6.1	4	1-1	2	4	3.98
Bair	2.2	0	0-0	0	1	3.05

INDIANS 6, TIGERS 4 *(Second game)*   71 – 33

PITCHER	IP	H	R-ER	BB	SO	ERA
Rozema (7-3)	2.1	7	6-4	0	0	3.43
Lopez	6.2	4	0-0	1	5	2.51

I like Garbey's natural swing more than Sparky does

Wednesday, August 1

INDIANS 4, TIGERS 2   71 — 34

PITCHER	IP	H	R-ER	BB	SO	ERA
Petry (14-5)	7.1	6	3-2	1	5	2.86
Hernandez	1.2	2	1-1	2	2	2.02

Thursday, August 2

TIGERS 2, INDIANS 1   72 — 34

PITCHER	IP	H	R-ER	BB	SO	ERA
Morris (14-7)	8.0	7	1-1	0	1	3.08
Hernandez (S22)	1.0	1	0-0	0	0	2.00

W E had three days to regroup after slumping into the All-
Star break. This time, we have only a matter of hours to
recover from a four-game sweep by the Kansas City Royals.

The most disconcerting aspect of our situation is that we
are headed to Boston for five games in three days, including
back-to-back doubleheaders. Our record is 72-38. Our lead
over the Toronto Blue Jays has shrunk to eight games for the
first time since July 20. We're not playing well. We're not pitching well. Our battle is over more than a slump or our opponents. We are also fighting the immense pressures of preserving
unprecedented early-season success. We've been on top since
Opening Day, and we've been the target of every other team
in the American League for the entire season.

There is an exclusive aura attached to teams that lead a
pennant race from Opening Day to the final day of the regular
season. We still qualify for that company, which is limited to
two teams—the 1923 New York Giants and the 1927 New York
Yankees.

Detroit is a tremendous baseball city, and the players are
reaping the financial benefits of the club's standing by making
personal appearances and filming television commercials, but
we must constantly remember that the other clubs are keying
on us. I have worked to correct what is in my opinion Sparky's
only fault. He talks so much about other clubs, other players,
and other managers with such brutally frank descriptions that
he's inspiring those people to beat us. I encourage Sparky to
restrict his discussions with the media to his own players. That
way no opposing players can put motivational newspaper clip-
pings on their bulletin board.

This next week will be an acid test. Fenway Park hasn't
been a paradise for us over the years. Boston's a better ballclub
in their own park than we are. The Red Sox key on the wall
better than we do. They have right-handed power hitters in
Evans, Rice, and Armas, all of whom can capitalize on the

Green Monster in left field, and they have lefties Mike Easler and Wade Boggs, who frequently hit to left-center field, where the Monster also comes into play.

There could be a bit of psychology involved. I know when I first arrived in Detroit the New York Yankees beat us at Yankee Stadium and Tiger Stadium because they were a much better ballclub. We expected to be beaten before the game even began. Sometimes I sense that feeling when we play in Boston.

The most demoralizing game of the Kansas City series was the opener of Sunday's doubleheader. Hernandez lost for the first time this season. The Royals beat us in their final at-bat. The winning hit, struck by Dane Iorg, was nothing more than a routine fly ball that landed short of the warning track in left field. Willie was victimized by Ruppert Jones, our left fielder, who positioned himself extremely shallow to eliminate any possible flare hit.

Dick Tracewski, who aligns our outfield defense, is a very conscientious coach. Sparky was upset about the alignment of Jones, and Trixie was hurt because he never makes mistakes of that nature. Ruppert merely snuck in on that pitch, and it cost us the game.

We were stunned, and that shock spilled over into the second game as the Royals scored four times in the first inning to complete the sweep. One small consolation was the fact that Juan Berenguer went the distance in defeat to allow our bullpen rest for the Boston series. Juan shut out the Royals over the final eight innings.

We geared up for the Red Sox by recalling pitcher Carl Willis to start the second game of Monday's doubleheader. Willis is a relief pitcher, but he is also the most rested and capable pitcher available to us from our Triple-A affiliate at Evansville. In this situation you don't ask for a specific pitcher. You want the pitcher who's ready to pitch that day.

This transaction is an example of the business side of baseball. Reserve outfielder Rusty Kuntz had to be optioned to Evansville to make room for Willis. Kuntz is a model player. He possesses as much enthusiasm and energy as any player I've known, and he approaches every day as if it's his last day in the major leagues. We will miss his enthusiasm.

Friday, August 3
ROYALS 9, TIGERS 6   72 – 35

PITCHER	IP	H	R-ER	BB	SO	ERA
Wilcox (11-7)	3.0	6	6-6	1	5	4.24
Lopez	6.0	5	3-2	0	5	2.54

Saturday, August 4
ROYALS 9, TIGERS 5   72 – 36

PITCHER	IP	H	R-ER	BB	SO	ERA
Abbott	5.1	8	4-4	0	1	6.02
Bair (4-3)	0.1	2	2-2	2	0	3.31
Monge	0.2	2	3-3	1	1	3.32
Lopez	1.2	3	0-0	0	1	2.50
Hernandez	1.0	0	0-0	1	2	1.98

Sunday, August 5
ROYALS 5, TIGERS 4 *(First game)*   72 – 37

PITCHER	IP	H	R-ER	BB	SO	ERA
Rozema	6.0	10	3-3	1	2	3.50
Hernandez (6-1)	3.0	6	2-2	0	1	2.11

ROYALS 4, TIGERS 0 *(Second game)*   72 – 38

PITCHER	IP	H	R-ER	BB	SO	ERA
Berenguer (5-8)	9.0	8	4-4	2	8	3.98

MONDAY, AUGUST 6   BOSTON

O UR pitchers took a beating and our earned run average soared, but the bottom line is that we were able to win one game of our twi-night doubleheader with the Boston Red Sox thanks to Lopez and Hernandez. My Latin Connection combined to allow only one run in four and one-third innings, and we captured the opening game 9-7. But Carl Willis was slammed for four runs in the first inning of a 10-2 defeat in the second game.

The opener looked like a cinch when Petry was armed with a 7-2 lead in the fifth inning, but Dan suffered through his poorest outing of the season. He consistently fell behind in the count and had problems with his slider. That left him with a fastball as his only weapon. He lapsed into the same type of negative thinking that victimized Wilcox on our first trip here in April, and Boston responded with four runs.

Aurelio saved our staff during doubleheaders

Lopez surrendered a solo home run to Rich Gedman in two and two-thirds innings to improve his record to 8-0. Hernandez allowed one harmless single over the final one and two-thirds innings to register his twenty-third save. Willie relied heavily on his screwball, which breaks down and away from right-handed hitters. This is a very effective pitch in Fenway Park because right-handed hitters attempt to clear the Green Monster. The pitch is enhanced by wasting good fastballs inside. A pitcher must bust some fastballs in on right-handed hitters at Fenway just to keep them from leaning over the plate for pitches away.

I don't believe I've ever met a man who can pitch as frequently and as long as Aurelio. He's pitched seventeen innings in the past seven days. Every day he comes to me and tells me he's available to pitch. That's precisely what we need at this point. He told me when I first joined the organization that he could pitch every day unless I was notified to the contrary.

Willis couldn't get untracked for his emergency start. He faced five batters and retired only one, but he didn't make any excuses. I feel a little sorry for him. Carl is a reliever and was placed in a precarious position when summoned to start. He told me after the game that he is ready to pitch tomorrow. That type of fortitude is going to carry us through this hectic period.

TIGERS 9, RED SOX 7 *(First game)*   73 – 38

PITCHER	IP	H	R-ER	BB	SO	ERA
Petry	4.2	10	6-4	2	2	3.00
Lopez (8-0)	2.2	4	1-1	2	3	2.53
Hernandez (S23)	1.2	1	0-0	0	1	2.07

RED SOX 10, TIGERS 2 *(Second game)*   73 – 39

PITCHER	IP	H	R-ER	BB	SO	ERA
Willis (0-2)	0.1	5	4-4	0	0	8.36
Bair	4.2	7	5-5	1	0	3.73
Monge	3.0	4	1-1	1	0	3.28

BOSTON is stomping my pitching staff. We lost the opener 12-7, as the Boston Red Sox clubbed a pair of grand slam home runs off Morris in the first two innings. We trailed in the second game, 5-4 in the ninth inning, and the scoreboard showed the Toronto Blue Jays leading the Texas Rangers by one run in the seventh inning. Our lead was ready to tumble to seven games.

We tied the second game in the ninth on a pinch-hit double by Dave Bergman and an error by first baseman Bill Buckner. We won in the eleventh on a two-run home run by Parrish. Lance has clubbed four homers in this pair of doubleheaders. Toronto lost. Our lead is secure.

Willie worked one inning for his twenty-fourth save, but the hero of this game and our stretch of doubleheaders is Aurelio. He worked three and one-third hitless innings to gain his ninth victory without defeat and run his innings pitched to twenty and one-third (three runs) in eight grueling days.

Aurelio doesn't throw in the bullpen as much as most relief pitchers. He and Willie engage in a pre-game form of catch much like Clem Labine used to when he served as a relief pitcher for the Brooklyn Dodgers. Aurelio and Willie will get about eighty feet apart and throw long to stretch their arms. They'll throw ten minutes—an excellent exercise for relief pitchers.

Latins seem to have a capacity to pitch frequently. The Latins play winter ball and aren't accustomed to resting their arms. I rested my arm every winter during my professional career. This is a mistake. If I were twenty years old, I'd live in California or Florida so I could throw during the off-season. I've heard Juan tell all kinds of stories about how he'd start one day and pitch nine innings, then come back the next day and pitch five innings in relief.

The thirty-five-year-old Aurelio is a sensitive person who

requires constant reminders of his value to the team. He says he wants to be traded after this season because he prefers the role now occupied by Willie. There is a certain amount of jealousy here. Aurelio voluntarily retired in September of 1982 for personal reasons one day after serving up four home runs in a starting assignment. That outing was an embarrassment for him. I feel his poor performance was the major reason he retired. He was hoping the Tigers would trade him and he wouldn't have to return to face the fans.

I consider Aurelio to be a personal friend and, potentially, a fine coach. When we hold our meetings prior to every series to review the opposing hitters, Lopez can dissect those hitters better than anyone on the club.

Aurelio reconsidered his retirement and returned to the Tigers in 1983. He recorded sixteen saves by the end of July, signed a two-year contract worth $1.2 million, and was rendered ineffective by gout. When the problem resurfaced early this season, Aurelio had to change his eating habits and refrain from drinking beer. So far, he has exercised a tremendous amount of self-discipline.

Aurelio was one of seven children. His father, Aurelio, Sr., supervised massive construction projects, including a canal through the jungles of Guatemala. Aurelio was constantly on the move. He acceded to his father's wish to get a college education and studied business law at the University of Puebla in Mexico. Later he persuaded his father to allow him to take a fling at professional baseball.

Aurelio toiled for eight years in the Mexican League before receiving an opportunity with the Kansas City Royals at the close of the 1974 season. The Royals cut him the following spring. He returned to the Mexican League until 1978, when the St. Louis Cardinals purchased his contract. The Tigers acquired Aurelio as a throw-in during the winter of 1978 in a deal that brought outfielder Jerry Morales to Detroit for pitchers Bob Sykes and Jack Murphy. Not a bad deal.

Wilcox started the second game and carried a 4-1 lead

into the seventh inning, when he lost the lead on home runs by Dwight Evans and Jim Rice. Evans and Rice both hit fastballs that Milt failed to throw inside far enough. This is the risk of pitching inside at Fenway. A small margin of error exists on that inside corner.

This was Jack's worst outing since I've been here. He didn't seem mentally prepared for the task at hand. I believe he remains bothered by the criticism he's received from teammates and myself. His mental preparation is my responsibility. I have worked harder with this man this year than I've ever worked in my life. I've tried hard, but to no avail. I have to get him straightened out.

Our spate of doubleheaders is ended and any lingering doubts concerning our pennant capabilities have evaporated.

We are going to win this division.

RED SOX 12, TIGERS 7 *(First game)*   73 – 40

PITCHER	IP	H	R-ER	BB	SO	ERA
Morris (14-8)	1.1	6	9-8	2	2	3.48
Monge	4.2	6	3-3	1	1	3.71
Willis	2.0	1	0-0	1	0	7.31

TIGERS 7, RED SOX 5 *(Second game, 11 innings)* 74 – 40

PITCHER	IP	H	R-ER	BB	SO	ERA
Wilcox	6.2	9	5-5	1	5	4.36
Lopez (9-0)	3.1	0	0-0	0	5	2.44
Hernandez (S24)	1.0	0	0-0	0	2	2.05

W E ran out of gas about the same time we ran out of pitchers in losing the series finale to the Red Sox 8-0. Abbott failed to survive the first inning, just as Willis had on Monday. Our starting pitchers permitted twenty-nine runs in thirteen and two-thirds innings. I tip my cap to Berenguer despite today's defeat. Juan came back two days after pitching a complete game to provide our greatly taxed staff with five and one-third innings of relief.

This series reminded me of the 1960 World Series, in which the New York Yankees outscored the Pittsburgh Pirates 55-27 but lost in seven games. We were outscored here 42-25, but we're heading for Kansas City with the same eight-and-one-half-game lead we carried to Boston.

Willis was sent back to Evansville to make room for the return of rookie shortstop Doug Baker. Carl leaves with an 0-2 record and 7.31 earned run average. I still like him a lot as a middle reliever. He's fearless and he keeps the ball down in the strike zone.

The Red Sox appear to be the club to beat next season. They possess a lineup that disturbs most pitchers. Lee Stange has done a tremendous job of building a young and effective pitching staff, as evidenced by Dennis "Oil Can" Boyd's shutout victory today.

RED SOX 8, TIGERS 0   74 – 41

PITCHER	IP	H	R-ER	BB	SO	ERA
Abbott (3-4)	0.2	5	5-0	0	1	5.93
Berenguer	5.1	6	2-1	0	4	3.87
Rozema	2.0	3	1-1	1	1	3.53

W E became the only team to sweep the Kansas City Royals six games in the same season on their home artificial turf. Some people probably wonder how we could sweep the Royals in Kansas City and be swept by the Mariners on their artificially surfaced field at the Kingdome. One of the reasons is that we were fresh coming into Kansas City following an off-day.

Our visit to Seattle at the end of May presented a different set of circumstances. We were setting a terrific pace. We had won seventeen consecutive road games and our record was 35-5, a pace that is impossible to maintain. But our pitching didn't fail us here. Lopez won the opener 5-4 with a save to Hernandez and a game-winning home run by Ruppert Jones. Aurelio saved the second game for Morris 9-5 after Jack yielded three runs in the ninth inning. Wilcox provided us with six strong innings to claim the third game 8-4. We had desperately wanted Jack to pitch a complete game. He was coming off a bad outing in Boston. A complete-game victory can do wonders for a struggling pitcher.

Our lead over the Blue Jays now stands at nine games, thanks primarily to Aurelio and Willie. Aurelio had three wins and a save in four consecutive appearances on this road trip. They have combined for thirty-seven saves and sixteen victories in seventeen decisions to this point. That's a 53-1 mark, although there is some overlap. Aurelio has saved three of Willie's victories, while Willie has saved four of Aurelio's victories.

I had an opportunity to visit my nephew Lynn and his family before we left Kansas City for the annual Hall of Fame exhibition game at Cooperstown. My wife, Carolyn, made the trip to Kansas City and we grilled hamburgers in Lynn's backyard. I seized the opportunity to pitch to Lynn's three-year-old son, Jonathan, who had a nasty habit of stepping in the bucket, or pulling his front foot away from the pitch. I told him he shouldn't do that, but he persisted. I moved him to the edge of Lynn's swimming pool. The next time he stepped into the bucket he also stepped into the pool. He wasn't too happy, but he was cured of a bad habit.

Cooperstown was a mad rush on Monday. We had originally planned to leave Kansas City on Monday morning, but Sparky decided to depart on Sunday night. We flew into Utica and arrived at midnight. The following morning we took a bus to Cooperstown, which was a ninety-minute drive. We played the game, took the bus back to Utica, and finally arrived in Detroit at 9 P.M. Monday.

We defeated the Atlanta Braves 7-5, and I traded some memories with Billy Herman, who was my hitting instructor during my managerial days with the San Diego Padres.

Friday, August 10
TIGERS 5, ROYALS 4   75 – 41

PITCHER	IP	H	R-ER	BB	SO	ERA
Petry	6.2	7	4-4	2	5	3.09
Lopez (10-0)	1.1	1	0-0	1	0	2.41
Hernandez (S25)	1.0	0	0-0	0	0	2.03

Saturday, August 11
TIGERS 9, ROYALS 5   76 – 41

PITCHER	IP	H	R-ER	BB	SO	ERA
Morris (15-8)	8.2	11	5-5	0	4	3.57
Lopez (S12)	0.1	0	0-0	0	1	2.40

Sunday, August 12
TIGERS 8, ROYALS 4   77 – 41

PITCHER	IP	H	R-ER	BB	SO	ERA
Wilcox (12-7)	6.1	3	3-3	2	2	4.36
Lopez	0.2	2	1-1	0	1	2.47
Hernandez	2.0	1	0-0	0	0	1.99

WE lost a doubleheader to the California Angels 6-4 and 12-1. The Blue Jays moved to within seven and one-half games.

Sparky and I have decided to return to a four-man starting rotation. We have no more scheduled doubleheaders and enjoy the luxury of five off-days over the final six weeks of the season. We feel Morris, Petry, and Wilcox are capable starters.

Berenguer and Rozema were our starting pitchers in this doubleheader—a pitchoff to determine our fourth starter. Juan pitched well in the opener after permitting two runs in the first inning. Dave was not impressive in the second game. He was driven from the mound in a seven-run third inning.

Dave has no pop on his fastball. He is pushing one hundred innings for the season and that seems to be his maximum workload. He lacks strength and stamina and seems depressed. He's in the final year of a three-year contract, and his future is in a twilight zone. Doubts persist in Dave's mind: Am I going to be here next year? Where will I go? It would be nice for Dave's sake to tell him he will be with the Tigers for five more years, but that's not possible. There are always young pitchers coming up through farm systems to take the place of incumbents. There's still a spot for Dave on this club, but he'll have to earn it.

Juan is the antithesis of Dave. He's not a polished pitcher, but he leads our staff in arm strength, endurance, and perseverance. Juan was rejected by the Mets, the Royals, and the Blue Jays earlier in his career. Bill Lajoie signed him on a hunch one day after he was cut by the Blue Jays in the spring of 1982.

Hernandez suffered his second loss in tonight's opener. He got beat in the ninth inning when Doug DeCinces hit a screwball off the end of his bat for a bloop single. This type of game will eat at your brain. We were banking on our best pitcher with the game tied in the ninth inning.

We asked for waivers on Abbott so that we could give him his unconditional release. This move will help Glenn in the long run. He has an astute baseball mind and is capable of being a fine pitching coach.

ANGELS 6, TIGERS 4 *(First game)*   77 – 42

PITCHER	IP	H	R-ER	BB	SO	ERA
Berenguer	6.0	5	3-3	3	6	3.90
Lopez	1.0	2	1-1	1	0	2.53
Hernandez (6-2)	2.0	3	2-2	1	0	2.12

ANGELS 12, TIGERS 1 *(Second game)*   77 – 43

PITCHER	IP	H	R-ER	BB	SO	ERA
Rozema (7-4)	2.0	7	5-5	0	2	3.94
Bair	3.1	5	5-5	3	2	4.17
Monge	3.2	3	2-2	1	5	3.82

PETRY gave us eight strong innings in an 8-3 thrashing of the California Angels. That helped galvanize a tattered staff that had not permitted fewer than four runs in our previous fourteen games.

I have a strong affection for Dan, strong enough to have allowed him to date my youngest daughter, Vikki, a few years ago. He's a sensitive person and not a carouser. His only date on road trips is with the television set in his hotel room.

This game could have a tremendous impact on our season. The Toronto Blue Jays lost a doubleheader to the Cleveland Indians. Our lead is back to nine games.

TIGERS 8, ANGELS 3   78 – 43

PITCHER	IP	H	R-ER	BB	SO	ERA
Petry (15-5)	8.0	8	3-3	1	5	3.11
Hernandez	1.0	0	0-0	0	0	2.10

W E handed Morris a 5-0 lead after two innings and he blew it by the fourth. We rallied for an 8-7 victory in twelve innings because Bair, Lopez, and Hernandez managed to atone for Jack's bad performance with eight and one-third innings of scoreless relief. Jack is having problems, and I wish I could put my finger on the reason.

Kirk Gibson might be able to crawl into Jack's mind. Gibson entered the clubhouse gleefully following this victory and observed the forlorn figure of Jack slumped in front of his locker. "I'm not criticizing Jack for his performance," Kirk said later. "He didn't intentionally lose the lead. But we came into the clubhouse happy, and he was over in the corner pouting. He should have been the first one at the clubhouse door."

Sometimes players can communicate more effectively with other players than managers or coaches can. Gibson is a big cat who is not afraid to holler at opposing players, umpires, or teammates. You don't appoint captains. They surface. I made the mistake of appointing Dave Winfield as my captain when I managed the San Diego Padres. Winfield is a great player, but not a leader. My captain should have been Gene Tenace.

Jack was angered at Gibson's words, and told him so. We did discover after the game that Jack had been suffering from a viral infection that caused congestion in his head and chest. He was just too doggone proud to admit he was sick.

TIGERS 8, ANGELS 7 *(12 innings)*   79 – 43

PITCHER	IP	H	R-ER	BB	SO	ERA
Morris	3.2	9	7-7	4	4	3.84
Bair	3.1	1	0-0	3	0	3.99
Lopez	1.1	2	0-0	0	0	2.50
Hernandez (7-2)	3.2	0	0-0	0	6	2.03

U MPIRE Steve Palermo ejected Lou Whitaker for smiling. Sweet Lou would smile broadly each time he went to his position. Palermo interpreted Whitaker's smiles as a form of intimidation. What's with this guy? I thought Palermo was going to be a good umpire when I first saw him a few years ago, but he's been after us since he ruled a short-hopped fly ball an out in Chicago three years ago. That call resulted in a White Sox triple play. He tries to job us every time he has a chance. We attempt to steer clear of any confrontations involving Palermo, but it's a pretty sad commentary on his qualifications as an umpire. Sparky was so incensed that he had club president Jim Campbell phone Dick Butler, the supervisor of umpires, to lodge a complaint.

Wilcox, who has had his share of run-ins with Palermo, overcame a little wildness to defeat the Seattle Mariners 6-2 and claim his thirteenth victory. That matches Milt's career-high.

Alan Trammell provided the club with a lift by returning to shortstop for the first time since the All-Star break. Too bad he didn't get to play the entire game alongside his double-play partner, Whitaker.

Berenguer justified our faith in him by striking out twelve Mariners in a 4-3 victory on Saturday. His fastball was sizzling, and he did a good job of mixing in his curve and split-fingered fastball.

Hernandez came to Juan's rescue in a two-run Seattle ninth inning. Willie has twenty-six saves.

Petry lost on Sunday, 4-1, despite striking out a career-high eleven batters in going the distance. We managed only four hits off rookie left-hander Mark Langston, who is the best young pitcher I've seen since Dave Righetti emerged for the New York Yankees. Langston turns twenty-four on Monday.

How could anyone be upset with Whitaker's smile?

Friday, August 17

TIGERS 6, MARINERS 2   80 – 43

PITCHER	IP	H	R-ER	BB	SO	ERA
Wilcox (13-7)	8.0	7	1-1	3	5	4.19
Lopez	1.0	1	1-1	1	1	2.56

Saturday, August 18

TIGERS 4, MARINERS 3   81 – 43

PITCHER	IP	H	R-ER	BB	SO	ERA
Berenguer (6-8)	8.1	3	3-2	4	12	3.78
Hernandez (S26)	0.2	1	0-0	0	0	2.02

Sunday, August 19

MARINERS 4, TIGERS 1   81 – 44

PITCHER	IP	H	R-ER	BB	SO	ERA
Petry (15-6)	9.0	10	4-4	3	11	3.15

I sympathize with Jackie Moore, the manager of the Oakland A's. We swept his club by scores of 14-1, 12-6, and 11-4. The Toronto Blue Jays and the rest of the division are dots on the horizon.

Our starting pitchers—Jack Morris, Milt Wilcox, and Juan Berenguer—didn't experience any difficulty in recording victories as we outscored the A's 16-3 through the first three innings and 32-4 through six innings. The final three innings became inconsequential. We batted .395 and slugged .667 for the series. We used our license to steal in the final game against left-hander Bill Krueger. We stole six bases in as many attempts to run our season total to eleven without a failure when Krueger was on the mound.

I use a microcassette to compile a bank of data on opposing pitchers. Krueger has a high leg kick and a deliberate delivery to home plate. He also has a poor move to first base because he tips it off. He brings his lead leg behind the rubber during his windup when he's going to home plate, but makes an unnatural still motion when he goes to first base. Krueger's moves are more obvious than those of anyone else in the league. He's a lot like Len Barker, who was "run" to the National League.

The A's staff was in such a shambles that Moore used utility infield Mark Wagner to pitch one and two-thirds innings of Monday night's opening game. Moore didn't want to waste an arm. I don't see anything wrong with that. We almost used catcher/third baseman Marty Castillo during our siege of doubleheaders.

I was faced with a similar situation in 1968 when I managed Albuquerque. The opposition was murdering my staff. I strolled from the dugout to the mound, even though I wasn't on the active roster, and pitched a couple of innings. Sometimes you have no choice.

Monday, August 20

TIGERS 14, A's 1   82 — 44

PITCHER	IP	H	R-ER	BB	SO	ERA
Morris (16-8)	7.0	3	1-1	3	6	3.75
Rozema	2.0	2	0-0	0	2	3.86

Tuesday, August 21

TIGERS 12, A's 6   83 — 44

PITCHER	IP	H	R-ER	BB	SO	ERA
Wilcox (14-7)	6.0	4	2-2	0	7	4.15
Bair	1.0	2	0-0	0	0	3.94
Lopez	1.0	2	2-2	2	1	2.69
Hernandez	1.0	3	2-2	0	0	2.16

Wednesday, August 22

TIGERS 11, A's 4   84 — 44

PITCHER	IP	H	R-ER	BB	SO	ERA
Berenguer (7-8)	7.0	5	1-1	2	1	3.65
Bair	1.0	2	2-1	0	0	4.00
Monge	1.0	2	1-1	1	1	3.97

A NAHEIM brings out the best in the Tigers. I think it's show-manship. We're always a good draw for the California An-gels. Management appreciates our appeal, even if the Angels players don't. We won two of three games.

The turnout of Tiger fans here continues to surprise me. This is the toughest park in the league for members of our team to acquire good seat locations for their friends and rel-atives. The demand for tickets is overwhelming. The clubhouse always looks like a lottery ticket window when the players crowd around traveling secretary Bill Brown to place their orders.

Some of our players played at Anaheim Stadium before signing professional contracts. Parrish, for example, who lives in nearby Yorba Linda, was run through a tryout here by an-other team before being drafted by the Tigers on the first round in 1974. Petry lives in the shadows of Anaheim Stadium and has enjoyed good success here. He wavered on Friday, how-ever, in a 5-3 complete-game defeat. He had difficulty getting loose, and the Angels capitalized on it, scoring four runs in the first inning.

Dan is complaining of shoulder stiffness. Many pitchers experience this in the latter stages of a season. We will have to ease back a bit on his throwing between starts and especially avoid the slider.

Morris turned in a good eight-inning performance in his 5-1 victory on Saturday. Jack seems to have regained his slider. The snap is back after I convinced him to grip the pitch across the seams, which allows him to throw the ball harder.

Wilcox won his fifteenth game and fourth consecutive start on Sunday, 12-6. He worked six innings on a yield of three unearned runs, using a good fastball to limit the Angels to five hits while recording five strikeouts. Milt's fastball grip is different from that of most pitchers. He holds the ball a little off center. The pitch reacts like a little bitty slider. Milt also uses a knuckle-curve as a good weapon. He places his index finger on top of the ball to get better spin and a tighter rotation. The pitch is similar to Don Sutton's curve, one of the best in the league.

I was not pleased with Bair's performance. He allowed four hits and three runs in one and two-thirds innings. He has fallen into a bad habit of failing to use the fastball—his best pitch—to put away batters. Doug often gets ahead in the count and then tries to finesse batters instead of going after them aggressively. I don't understand that thinking.

Friday, August 24
ANGELS 5, TIGERS 3   84 – 45

PITCHER	IP	H	R-ER	BB	SO	ERA
Petry (15-7)	8.0	6	5-5	3	3	3.25

Saturday, August 25
TIGERS 5, ANGELS 1   85 – 45

PITCHER	IP	H	R-ER	BB	SO	ERA
Morris (17-8)	8.0	9	1-1	5	4	3.64
Hernandez	1.0	0	0-0	0	1	2.14

Sunday, August 26
TIGERS 12, ANGELS 6   86 – 45

PITCHER	IP	H	R-ER	BB	SO	ERA
Wilcox (15-7)	6.0	5	3-0	0	5	4.00
Bair	1.2	4	3-2	2	1	4.15
Lopez	1.1	0	0-0	0	1	2.66

AUGUST 28-30   SEATTLE

T HE Tigers have added another pupil to my class. We have acquired left-handed reliever Bill Scherrer from the Cincinnati Reds organization. I promptly dispatched him to the bullpen for observation.

Bill is a bony twenty-six-year-old who stands six-foot-four. He has pretty good pop on his fastball and an outstanding curve, although he threw a bad one that will cost us the services of Dave Bergman for a few days. Sparky had summoned Bergman to emulate a batter as Scherrer warmed up. A curve got away from Bill, and Dave had to twist out of the way to avoid being hit in the head. He strained some muscles in his lower back doing it and has joined Chet Lemon on the bench. Chet lost a fly ball in the sun on Sunday in Anaheim and was struck on the head. He is suffering from vertigo and didn't report to the Kingdome on Tuesday. Lemon and Bergman are two of our finest defensive players. My staff and I hope they aren't incapacitated for long.

Bill Scherrer, the latest addition to my pitching class

We won one of three games here. I suppose we should feel fortunate. The Kingdome has had a curse on us over the years. We lost five of six games here this season. Our 5-1 loss on Wednesday can be explained in two words: Mark Langston. We hit only four balls out of the infield (two for singles) and struck out twelve times in succumbing to Mark's smoking fastballs and crackling slider. Tossing the slider, he reminds me of a young Ron Guidry. Coaches Dick Tracewski and Alex Grammas feel Langston throws as hard as Sandy Koufax in his heyday with the Los Angeles Dodgers. I don't necessarily agree, but I can't deny my envy of Langston. I know one staff that could use a left-handed starting pitcher of his capabilities.

We did prevail in the series opener, and Scherrer played a vital role. Berenguer started and was victimized by three unearned runs in the seventh inning to fall behind 4-1. Scherrer prevented further damage by retiring left-handed hitting Alvin Davis on a groundout, stranding two runners. We rallied to win 5-4 on the strength of a game-winning double by Ruppert Jones and two innings of scoreless relief from Hernandez.

I leave Seattle with concerns about Petry and Morris, my two top starters. Dan lost to Langston and allowed ten hits in four and one-third innings. He had a decent fastball but didn't use it enough and didn't use it properly. He has to bring that fastball inside to prevent hitters from leaning to reach the outside fastball. Dan argued that he was throwing good pitches on the outside corner. But those pitches are good only if you keep the hitters honest. A pitcher has to treasure the entire width of home plate: he has to work with all seventeen inches of it. I'm having an extremely difficult time hammering home this point to Petry.

Jack deserves high grades for his pitching in a 2-1 loss on Thursday, but failing grades for his conduct. He was locked in a scoreless game when he walked Spike Owen on four pitches to open the eighth inning. He returned the ball to home plate in disgust. Lance Parrish never saw it, and the ball went back to the screen. Time was not called. Home plate umpire Durwood Merrill looked around in astonishment. Fortunately, an unwitting Owen didn't seize the opportunity to scamper to second. When play was resumed, Jack threw a Jack Perconte bunt into right field. Both runners scored on the play when Gibson overthrew Parrish and Jack wasn't backing up the throw. Trammell retrieved the ball and returned it to Jack, who jerked it out of Trammell's hand. That was an embarrassment to Trammell.

I talked to Jack the following day about his fundamental oversight but not his behavior. Jack seems to dig in deeper when his temper is discussed. His tantrums are a reflex action. He can't control them. We don't like it, but can't take the ball from the hands of the man who is supposed to be our best starting pitcher. This is frustrating.

Tuesday, August 28

TIGERS 5, MARINERS 4   87 – 45

PITCHER	IP	H	R-ER	BB	SO	ERA
Berenguer	6.2	5	4-1	4	5	3.54
Scherrer	0.1	0	0-0	0	0	0.00
Hernandez (8-2)	2.0	1	0-0	0	1	2.11

Wednesday, August 29

MARINERS 5, TIGERS 1   87 – 46

PITCHER	IP	H	R-ER	BB	SO	ERA
Petry (15-8)	4.1	10	5-5	0	1	3.40
Rozema	2.2	1	0-0	0	1	3.75
Lopez	1.0	0	0-0	0	1	2.64

Thursday, August 30

MARINERS 2, TIGERS 1   87 – 47

PITCHER	IP	H	R-ER	BB	SO	ERA
Morris (17-9)	8.0	4	2-1	3	8	3.54

WILLIE? Won't he! Every time we've stumbled this season Hernandez has been there to pick us up. He did that Sunday in the final game of the series after we had lost the first two. Willie worked two perfect innings to save a 6-3 victory for Petry and snap our losing streak at four games. This is the third time we have lost four consecutive games, and Willie has saved the victory that followed each mini-slump. He now has twenty-seven saves in as many opportunities. Where would we be without him? I doubt we would be in first place. Dan really struggled for this victory: he allowed eleven hits and had no strikeouts in five and one-third innings before relinquishing duties to Aurelio and Willie. He can't shake his shoulder stiffness, and his pitching has suffered; his two best pitches, fastball and slider, are not anywhere near peak efficiency.

The first two games of this series were disconcerting. We lost the opener 7-6 in thirteen innings on a wild pitch by Dave Rozema. Wilcox had started but left in the fourth inning complaining of shoulder problems; it looks as if he will miss his next start on Tuesday in Detroit against the Orioles. He is expected to receive his fourth cortisone shot on Monday.

The second game was decided before anyone on the bench was comfortably seated. Berenguer was tagged for six runs in the first inning, the final three on a home run by Mike Davis. He had a two-strike count on Davis, shook off Parrish on a fastball and slider, and opted for a split-fingered fastball. He was wrong—you don't throw your third best pitch three runs down with two runners on base. One encouraging note was that Bair, who had been guilty of the same mistake in recent appearances, more closely resembled the power pitcher he is in checking the A's for three and two-thirds innings. Bill Scherrer allowed one run in the final three and two-thirds innings as we scrapped back, but fell short, 7-5.

Friday, August 31
A's 7, TIGERS 6 *(13 innings)*   87 – 48

PITCHER	IP	H	R-ER	BB	SO	ERA
Wilcox	3.2	4	5-4	5	1	4.12
Lopez	4.2	1	1-1	3	4	2.61
Hernandez	3.2	2	0-0	0	4	2.04
Rozema (7-5)	0.2	2	1-1	0	0	3.82

Saturday, September 1
A's 7, TIGERS 5   87 – 49

PITCHER	IP	H	R-ER	BB	SO	ERA
Berenguer (7-9)	0.2	3	6-6	3	1	3.91
Bair	3.2	4	0-0	3	4	3.96
Scherrer	3.2	2	1-1	1	3	2.25

Sunday, September 2
TIGERS 6, A's 3   88 – 49

PITCHER	IP	H	R-ER	BB	SO	ERA
Petry (16-8)	5.1	11	3-3	0	0	3.45
Lopez	1.2	1	0-0	0	1	2.57
Hernandez (S27)	2.0	0	0-0	0	0	2.01

MONDAY, SEPTEMBER 3   DETROIT

A crowd of 36,797 at Tiger Stadium witnessed a baseball oddity tonight. Morris was removed from a tie game in the eighth inning. I can't ever remember Jack being lifted in that situation. He had walked the bases loaded, and with two outs Sparky decided to bring in Lopez, who yielded a grand slam to Mike Young. Baltimore won 7-4.

The media pressed for answers. Why was Jack removed? It wasn't an easy move for Sparky to make, but Jack had thrown 128 pitches and was running on empty. Aurelio had been pitching well, so Sparky and I decided that he was our best bet. Jack might have reacted strongly but he had showered and left the park by the time we got into the clubhouse. I think Sparky's move, along with media criticism stemming from Jack's outburst in Seattle, has humbled Jack a bit. He didn't like what he read in the local papers when we returned from the West Coast. I think he finally realizes he can't avoid the press, and I expect a change in him soon.

We entered this series without the services of Lemon and Bergman, and tonight we lost Gibson to an intestinal virus. Those three will probably be out until we play the Blue Jays in Toronto on Friday. Their absence restricts Sparky's player maneuverability, but we'll just have to fill in and grind it out.

ORIOLES 7, TIGERS 4   88 – 50

PITCHER	IP	H	R-ER	BB	SO	ERA
Morris (17-10)	7.2	9	6-6	4	4	3.67
Lopez	0.0	2	1-1	0	0	2.65
Scherrer	0.2	2	0-0	0	1	1.93
Bair	0.2	0	0-0	0	0	3.93

TUESDAY, SEPTEMBER 4   DETROIT

WE lost a game to the Orioles and a game in the standings to the Blue Jays, but we might have gained a starting pitcher. Rookie right-hander Roger Mason, one of six players we recalled from Evansville, had a pretty fair major league debut. He had impressed me in spring training, and I suggested to Sparky that we start him tonight instead of Rozema. Although Roger had a good season at Evansville and was rested, Sparky preferred Rozie. Dave departed after allowing two runs in one-third of an inning, though, and Roger pitched the final eight innings. Even though we were beaten, 4-1, Roger's performance was a dream come true. He is a native of Michigan and is trying to break into the major leagues at the rather advanced age of twenty-five. I worked with him in the bullpen prior to the game to correct his grip of the split-fingered fastball—the results were instant. Roger struck out six Orioles in using the split-fingered fastball effectively.

We have lost six of our past seven games and our lead has been slashed to seven and one-half games over Toronto. There is no sign of panic, but we definitely could use a well-pitched game. I also wouldn't mind seeing Hernandez pitch because that means we have an awfully good chance of winning. Willie has appeared just twice in our past seven games.

Jack finally broke his silence. Sparky talked to him and persuaded him that that's what he ought to do. I could detect an immediate change in his personality; he is no longer distant and has, in a figurative sense, rejoined the club. Jack seems happy. I know I am; I only have to speak for myself.

ORIOLES 4, TIGERS 1   88 – 51

PITCHER	IP	H	R-ER	BB	SO	ERA
Rozema (7-6)	0.1	3	2-1	0	0	3.90
Scherrer	0.2	0	0-0	1	1	1.69
Mason	8.0	5	2-2	3	6	2.25

C HAMPIONSHIP teams require championship pitching. Ber-enguer and Hernandez beat Baltimore on three hits. Juan protected our first-inning run into the eighth when Willie slammed the door for the Tigers' first 1-0 victory since Dan Petry defeated the Chicago White Sox by that score on July 20, 1982. Juan never looked better; he had an outstanding fastball, and also threw his split-fingered fastball and curve often. We worked diligently on his curve a couple of days ago. He wasn't getting on top of the pitch enough and was lacking the good downward spin necessary to make the pitch effective. He threw both his breaking pitches when behind in the count tonight to thoroughly baffle the Orioles.

Berenguer showed championship stuff by shutting out the Orioles

Gibson and Lemon are mentally tough

We desperately needed this victory heading to Toronto. The absence of Lemon, Gibson, and Bergman stripped our offense of much of its ammunition. Juan sensed the urgency for victory, and I further encouraged him between innings to be aggressive and continue to throw his three pitches as long as he had command of them. And he was in command. He credited Lopey with helping him formulate a sound game plan: "He said to be careful with the big power hitters—Eddie Murray, Cal Ripken, and Wayne Gross—but to go after the rest." Thank you, coach Lopez.

TIGERS 1, ORIOLES 0   89 – 51

PITCHER	IP	H	R-ER	BB	SO	ERA
Berenguer (8-9)	7.1	2	0-0	3	7	3.72
Hernandez (S28)	1.2	1	0-0	1	1	1.98

THIS game will stick in the Blue Jays' craw when our champagne finally flows. We battled back from a 4-0 deficit in the eighth inning tonight and won in the tenth, 7-4, on a three-run home run by Dave Bergman off reliever Ron Musselman. Our entire team was overcome with joy and relief. "Smile, smile," shouted Darrell Evans. Sparky was as happy as I've ever seen him. "I wanted this game more than any I've ever managed," he declared, vowing to get a good night's sleep for the first time in a long time. It was a great win for Sparky because this is his team—one that he has molded himself over the past five seasons—and tonight it took a big step toward the championship.

We had lost three consecutive series and six of nine games. We had been dealt a serious blow by the injuries to Lemon and Bergman and the illness of Kirk Gibson. Our spirits were sagging, our doubts increasing. Our relatively young players, only four of whom (Wilcox, Bair, Hernandez, and Bergman) have ever been involved in post-season play, are a little tense. You just can't tell how players will react to pressure until they've been through the grind. This game restored our confidence, though, and raised our lead over the Blue Jays to nine and one-half games after it had fallen from twelve and one-half to seven and one-half in a period of thirteen days.

No game, with the possible exception of the second game of the August 7 doubleheader in Boston, more clearly represents our entire season. We fought hard to erase a deficit, then placed our fortune in the hands of Hernandez, whom we call "The King" because of the manner in which he struts around. Willie is entitled to strut to his heart's content; today he pitched three scoreless innings to raise his record to 9-2.

In the bottom of the ninth Cliff Johnson reached with an infield single and was replaced by pinch-runner Ron Shepherd. Mitch Webster struck out attempting to advance Shepherd with a sacrifice bunt. We then faced a steal attempt, which, if successful, would put Shepherd in scoring position. I signalled from the bench for Willie to throw to first base. Shepherd returned to the base safely, but I detected him leaning toward second a bit. That was my tipoff. Soon after, he did try to steal, but I had already flashed the pitchout sign to Willie and Lance, and Shepherd was caught stealing. After the game, Sparky called me into his office and announced to the gathered media that I had won the game.

I estimate that we retire between forty and sixty runners per season by signalling from the dugout for pitchouts and throws to first base. There is one important factor: the pitcher should hesitate a couple of seconds after he assumes his set position from the stretch before throwing to first base. Bair and Lopez come to a set and throw to first without hesitation: they throw almost before the runner has stepped off the bag. This doesn't allow me any opportunity to observe the runner. I want that runner to get off the base and do something that will tip off a steal attempt.

A three-run home run by Gibson off Doyle Alexander triggered our comeback in the eighth inning. Toronto manager Bobby Cox is probably second-guessing himself for not summoning left-handed relief pitcher Jimmy Key. You can't blame Cox for staying in the dugout, though; his bullpen has been on a torch drive all season. This was Toronto's twenty-third loss in its opponents' final at-bat; on the other hand, we have lost only five games in our opponents' final at-bat.

Petry started and had neither good stuff nor good location. He's having problems with his slider, which I thought we had solved. I'm going to change his approach in his next start, in Baltimore. He has to be more aggressive and throw for the middle of the plate; he has been too tentative. That's not a winning style of pitching. But we'll see what happens; he should show improvement.

The sixth inning was significant. Dan allowed one-out singles to George Bell and Willie Aikens. We were already trailing, 4-0, and the game was about to blow up in our face. Playing percentages, we brought in left-hander Bill Scherrer to face left-handed hitting Ernie Whitt. Whitt struck out. Sparky then called on Bair, a right-hander, to face right-handed hitting Jesse Barfield. Barfield struck out.

A special night was made even more special when I received a call after the game announcing the birth of Roger Craig III. Champagne, anyone?

TIGERS 7, BLUE JAYS 4 *(10 innings)*   90 − 51

PITCHER	IP	H	R-ER	BB	SO	ERA
Petry	5.1	6	4-2	1	3	3.44
Scherrer	0.1	0	0-0	0	1	1.59
Bair	1.1	0	0-0	0	1	3.87
Hernandez (9-2)	3.0	1	0-0	1	2	1.93

CRITICAL reports about the Tigers have been circulating for about three weeks. Twins manager Billy Gardner, for instance, was quoted as saying that the Blue Jays are better than the Tigers. We'll keep that clipping just in case Minnesota is our playoff opponent. Many people have stated that Toronto would have a substantial lead if they had Willie Hernandez. Well, they had the same chance we did in spring training, but refused to part with outfielder Jesse Barfield. Could've, would've, and should've have no place in baseball's dictionary. The rest of the American League can only wonder "what if?" We've got all the answers.

Morris had to be removed from the game in the fifth inning because of some stiffness in his pitching shoulder. I learned of the injury through a chain of players. Wilcox came to me as Jack walked to the mound in the fifth inning. "Watch Jack," he told me. "His arm is stiff." Gibson had asked Jack earlier how he felt, and Jack mentioned a little stiffness and a little twinge but rejected Gibson's recommendation to tell me. I told Sparky, who was inclined to wait until the half-inning had ended. Jack wasn't throwing extremely well, but still looked pretty good. I urged immediate action because we would have been responsible for any further injury. I walked to the mound after Jack had retired the first batter and bluntly asked how his arm felt. When he responded, "It's a little stiff and there's a little twinge," I didn't hesitate. He was gone.

We used Scherrer and Lopez to finish the game—a 10-4 win. Scherrer received credit for his first Tiger victory with another yeoman performance—three strikeouts in one and two-thirds innings. He looks like another good acquisition. As much as I liked Carl Willis, Scherrer is the one we need now—he's more advanced as a pitcher and there is a shortage of left-handers in our system. He must be a collector of rabbit's feet and four-leaf clovers; he toiled for six years in the minor league system of the Cincinnati Reds and couldn't find a spot on a team going nowhere. Now he's on the best team Baseball '84 has to offer. Lopez allowed two harmless runs over the final three innings. He used our big lead to experiment with a sinking fastball, which is not recommended on the artificial surface of Exhibition Stadium.

TIGERS 10, BLUE JAYS 4   91 – 51

PITCHER	IP	H	R-ER	BB	SO	ERA
Morris	4.1	5	2-2	1	2	3.68
Scherrer (1-0)	1.2	0	0-0	1	3	1.23
Lopez (S13)	3.0	5	2-2	1	2	2.73

I don't want to sound like I'm gloating, but the race is over. We completed a three-game sweep of the Toronto Blue Jays, who are fading out of our rearview mirror.

Gibson delivered the knockout punch in our 7-2 victory with a prodigious three-run home run on the first pitch from reliever Bryan Clark in the seventh inning. Chet Lemon was sitting beside me in the dugout, and as the ball soared over the right field wall Lemon said, "Well, that's it Toronto." Our lead over the Blue Jays is now a commanding eleven and one-half games, and the magic number for Detroit's first championship in twelve years is nine. "The season," said Darrell Evans, "is suddenly very short." We can take a tremendous amount of pride in our performance here this weekend—the Blue Jays had the best home record in the league when we arrived.

Three reasons we're on top – Jones, Brookens, and Evans

I think it's odd that everyone expects the players to show emotion. The fans may be near hysteria, but baseball is still our job. We aren't just "kids" romping in double knits to pass the time. I don't think the Blue Jays would have appreciated a celebration on their field today. We won three big games here, but the Jays aren't eliminated yet. Many reporters seem miffed, though; they expected us to dance a little jig or make outlandish statements to the effect that the rest of the East Division is a wasteland. We have to be tactful about our position. It's hard not to speak out because there is a tremendous sense of anticipation and excitement. But our project is not completed. This is the time to control emotion.

The victory was Wilcox's sixteenth. He didn't issue any walks in six innings and mixed his curveball and split-fingered fastball with a fastball that had enough zip to keep Toronto's hitters off stride. Some pitchers are little more than hard throwers, but Milt is a pitcher who knows how to exploit a hitter's weaknesses and recognizes the value of changing speeds to destroy a hitter's timing.

We used Willie the final two innings with a five-run lead because we want to stash every game possible into the win column.

TIGERS 7, BLUE JAYS 2   92 – 51

PITCHER	IP	H	R-ER	BB	SO	ERA
Wilcox (16-7)	6.0	8	2-2	0	5	4.08
Scherrer	1.0	0	0-0	0	0	1.08
Hernandez	2.0	0	0-0	0	1	1.90

M IKE Flanagan, a Cy Young award winner in 1979, became
   the only starting pitcher to beat us three times, leading
the Orioles to a 3-1 victory. He was the whole show in recording
his fourth complete game against us. In those four games, he
has permitted only two earned runs.

On the bench during games such as this one, Sparky and
I or one of the other coaches will implore the players to get
into the game. "C'mon, let's have some life on the bench," is
a popular phrase. The problem is that life on the bench is
created by baserunners and runs. Flanagan, a mature left-
handed pitcher, gave us no opportunity to come to life.

Berenguer pitched very well in the loss. Once again he
was the victim of sub-par offensive support—something that
has dogged him all season. He is 8-10 with a 3.66 earned run
average. The club has averaged 4.4 runs in each of the games
Juan has started. Milt Wilcox, by comparison, is 16-7 with a
4.08 earned run average and has received an average of 6.3
runs in each of his starts. Juan was very dejected after the
game; he had allowed only two runs in seven innings. He sat
by himself, only occasionally raising his head to sip a beer. I
tried to console him by telling him he had given us a chance
to win. "But I no win," he replied. "I want to win for the club."
I told him we couldn't ask any more of him than we had received and encouraged him to find a nice restaurant, have a
decent meal, and be ready for his next start.

Juan has made significant strides since the All-Star break.
He dearly wants recognition from his peers; he'll receive it if he
can conquer the problems he frequently experiences in the
first inning.

Tonight he loaded the bases with no outs. I went to the
mound as Eddie Murray and his twenty-one-game hitting streak
strolled to the plate. Juan had been squeezing the ball, indi-
cating that he was trying too hard and robbing him of velocity.
I instructed him to relax and go with his best fastballs down

the middle of the plate. He got Murray to ground into a double play, limiting the Orioles to only one run. Ray Miller, the pitching coach of the Orioles, later informed us that Juan's fastball was clocked at ninety-four miles per hour on their radar gun—that's dealing. The average major league fastball runs between eighty-six and eighty-eight miles per hour. I think Juan's problems will be diminished if he powers the ball and approaches the first inning as if it was the ninth.

ORIOLES 3, TIGERS 1   92 – 52

PITCHER	IP	H	R-ER	BB	SO	ERA
Berenguer (8-10)	7.0	5	2-2	4	3	3.66
Lopez	1.0	1	1-1	1	1	2.78

D AN Petry tries to be too cute at times. He wants to be a perfectionist, which shouldn't be his major concern at the age of twenty-five and armed with a solid fastball. He found himself in a one-out, bases-loaded situation in the first inning tonight, which prompted my visit to the mound. He was a little discouraged; he has been worrying about his pitching effectiveness for nearly a month and about some shoulder stiffness that won't go away. I gave Dan the same advice I gave Juan Berenguer the night before: I told him not to pitch tentatively, reinforcing the notion that he can throw ninety mile per hour fastballs down the middle of the plate. He's much more effective doing that than throwing eighty-five mile per hour fastballs on the corners.

That made him more aggressive; he struck out John Lowenstein and retired Ken Singleton on a fielder's choice to set the tone for our 9-2 conquest of the Orioles. We removed him in the seventh inning after he had thrown 118 pitches, including a home run pitch to Rick Dempsey in the fifth inning at a time when we led, 5-0. I told Dan he had thrown a good pitch to Dempsey. "What do you mean?" he asked. "It was a home run." From his point of view it was a bad pitch, but the cardinal sin of any pitcher given a five-run lead is to issue bases on balls. The idea is to throw strikes and give the batter a chance to hit the ball so someone can catch it—that's why we have eight defensive players. The percentages are very low that the batter will hit a home run. Even the best hitters in baseball history manage home runs only once every fifteen at-bats. Pitchers can be more effective if they use these odds.

Ralph Rowe, the batting instructor of the Orioles, commented that Petry's slider was one of the best he's seen this season. I thought it was very average. He's stiff-wristing the pitch and guiding it, rather than releasing the pitch with a fluid motion.

Bair replaced Dan and worked one and one-third scoreless innings but pulled a muscle on his right side and will be lost for about a week. We handed the ball to Hernandez for one inning tonight to ensure that he remains sharp. He retired three consecutive batters and now has not allowed a run his past sixteen and one-third innings.

Roger Mason makes his major league debut as a starting pitcher here tomorrow night. He is experiencing the normal anxieties—and then some. He has had three days to think about his start. That's a lot of time before facing the reigning World Champions. Roger is a native of Bellaire, Michigan, and attended Saginaw Valley State College. He is being swamped by calls and telegrams from friends and family wishing him good luck; one writer asked permission to watch Roger throw in the bullpen yesterday. Tomorrow's game is being broadcast and telecast to Michigan, and on Thursday, Roger's name will appear in every paper in Michigan.

These are added pressures that don't exist in the minor leagues. The situation requires a strong-minded athlete who can block out distractions and draw on his minor league preparation for a once-in-a-lifetime experience. Roger seems ready.

TIGERS 9, ORIOLES 2   93 – 52

PITCHER	IP	H	R-ER	BB	SO	ERA
Petry (17-8)	6.2	5	2-2	4	6	3.42
Bair	1.1	1	0-0	0	0	3.81
Hernandez	1.0	0	0-0	0	0	1.89

RAY Miller and Jimmy Williams, who are members of the Orioles coaching staff, congratulated us on a great season and wished us luck in the American League Championship Series and the World Series. This marked the first time any opposing player or coach had conceded the pennant to us. It meant a great deal coming from representatives of the World Champions.

Mason did not pitch the type of game he had hoped for; he allowed three runs in four innings in losing to Dennis Martinez, 3-1. Mason consistently fell behind in the count and didn't have control of his fastball.

Randy O'Neal, who was recalled from Evansville on September 1 when rosters were expanded to as many as forty players, provided us with three scoreless innings in relief. O'Neal has the best split-fingered fastball on the staff. I introduced him to the pitch in spring training and he has proved to be a fast learner. He did have a problem tipping off the pitch to the batters, though. He raised his right wrist when spreading his fingers to grip the pitch. That problem was alleviated by the use of a larger glove. O'Neal definitely fits into Tiger plans next season, along with Mason.

Martinez pitched extremely well. I can't figure this guy out. His record is 6-7, but should be much better based on the changeup and curveball he showed us tonight. I'll let Ray Miller, the Orioles pitching coach, worry about that.

My wife and I spent Thursday, an off-day, at Tom Brookens's farm in Federal, Pennsylvania. When we returned to Detroit on Thursday night, we discovered that our condominium had been burglarized. The thief took only two objects—a baseball autographed by Jack Morris on the day he pitched his no-hit game against the Chicago White Sox, and five Tiger T-shirts we had planned to send to our daughters. They did not touch more valuable objects. A policeman investigating the crime

Randy O'Neal became our most acclaimed rookie pitcher since Fidrych

said, "If you guys weren't playing so well, the vandalism wouldn't be so bad."

ORIOLES 3, TIGERS 1   93 – 53

PITCHER	IP	H	R-ER	BB	SO	ERA
Mason (0-1)	4.0	6	3-3	2	3	3.75
O'Neal	3.0	1	0-0	1	2	0.00
Scherrer	1.0	1	0-0	1	2	0.96

THERE will be no pennant celebration here this weekend. We had to sweep a three-game series from the Blue Jays, but lost the opener, 7-2. Morris continued to pitch ineffectively. He surrendered two home runs to Willie Aikens on high fastballs, and one home run to Ernie Whitt on a slider. He is not throwing his split-fingered fastball for strikes, either, which allows hitters to sit on his other pitches. His pitching has a lot of problems right now. Dave Rozema was a bright spot in this game. Dave pitched two strong innings, pitching with intensity, and his fastball was sinking.

I cannot avoid thinking about potential opponents in the playoffs. The Twins, Royals, and Angels are in a race that seems certain to go to the final day or two. I would prefer to play the Twins, who are predominantly a right-handed hitting team. That is a good matchup for us because we're predominantly a right-handed pitching team. California is a veteran team with some good left-handed hitters: Reggie Jackson, Fred Lynn, and Rod Carew. I think those mature players would rise to the occasion in the playoffs. Kansas City is the club I fear the most. They have speed in Willie Wilson, a game-breaking bat in the hands of George Brett, a stopper in the bullpen in Dan Quisenberry, and good, young, front-line pitching. Wilson is an amazing weapon. I'm more aware of that than anyone because I key on potential basestealers. If Wilson hits a ball in the gap, it's a triple. If he gets on first base, it's virtually a double because of his ability to steal. I'll take the Twins, even though they have improved over last year.

We use scouting reports and our own knowledge to determine how to pitch all of our opponents. That approach varies slightly depending on our starting pitcher. Here's an idea of how Dan Petry would pitch the Twins if they were our playoff opponent.

Kirby Puckett—Bunts at least once each game, so be on your toes. Good line drive hitter up the middle and can steal. High fastball hitter who doesn't like breaking balls down and away. Dan's slider should be effective on Kirby. He's a first-strike hitter, so we like to start him off with a breaking pitch.

Darrell Brown/Mickey Hatcher—Both high fastball hitters. Brown has to be jammed, which has been a problem for Dan. Hatcher gets sliders down.

Kent Hrbek—Has a blind spot up and in, but Dan has to get the pitch inside with some zip. Likes pitches middle of the plate and in. Don't throw Hrbek fastballs for strikes. Stay off the plate with fastballs. Use off-speed pitches, especially low and away.

Randy Bush—Dead fastball hitter, and prefers low fastballs. Dead pull hitter. Throw a lot of breaking pitches. Nothing too good on first pitch.

Tom Brunansky—Jam him with fastballs up and in, then change the speeds down and away. Good power to all fields. Play him straightaway.

Gary Gaetti—Dead pull hitter. Likes inside fastballs. Doesn't run well. Keep pitches down to increase chances for ground balls.

Tim Laudner—Fastball hitter with good power. Keep the fastball up and in. He likes it down.

Tim Teufel—Jumps on high, inside fastballs. Stay away with pitches.

BLUE JAYS 7, TIGERS 2   93 – 54

PITCHER	IP	H	R-ER	BB	SO	ERA
Morris (17-11)	6.0	7	5-5	3	1	3.78
Scherrer	1.0	1	2-2	3	0	2.61
Rozema	2.0	0	0-0	1	1	3.82

THE headlines read Ruppert Jones 2, Blue Jays 1. That was true—unless you're the pitching coach of the Tigers. We defeated the Blue Jays to whittle our magic number to four. Jones contributed mightily by leaping to rob Cliff Johnson of a game-tying home run in the eighth inning. Jones also hit a fourth-inning homer off Dave Stieb, whom I consider to be the best right-handed pitcher in the league at this point. That hit turned out to be a game winner.

I cannot say enough about Milt Wilcox and Willie Hernandez. Milt won his sixth straight game and ninth in the past ten to join Morris and Petry as seventeen-game winners. Willie pitched two scoreless innings—after awakening from his snooze—to register his twenty-ninth save in as many opportunities. Milt allowed only one hit in seven innings, a second-inning home run by George Bell on a 2-0 fastball. That mistake signalled a change in Milt's pitching pattern. He reverted to his split-fingered fastball or rapidly improving curve the few times he fell behind in the count to schackle the Blue Jays for the second time in seven days and record a season-high eight strikeouts.

Milt had told me in spring training that if he won fifteen games he'd buy me a jeep as a gesture of appreciation for all the help I've been to him over the years. When he won his fifteenth game I noticed he avoided me when at all possible. I called him aside and told him he didn't have to buy me anything. My reward was watching him rack up victories. Milt said he felt bad about not fulfilling his promise. I'll settle for victories and a ride to the World Series.

TIGERS 2, BLUE JAYS 1   94 – 54

PITCHER	IP	H	R-ER	BB	SO	ERA
Wilcox (17-7)	7.0	1	1-1	1	8	3.98
Hernandez (S29)	2.0	2	0-0	0	2	1.86

THIS was a bittersweet day. We soundly defeated Toronto 8-3 to pare our magic number to two and to relentlessly approach the inevitable zero.

I was hurt, however, by Jack Morris. Today was Jack's turn to throw between starting assignments, but he refused. I said I had some ideas about how to improve his slider and split-fingered fastball. He repeated that he didn't want to throw, and walked away. "Don't you want me to help you?" I asked. His response was, "I don't want to throw." I could have forced Jack to throw, but that would have been a waste of time. The throwing would not have been beneficial. I left him alone. He's hard-headed and takes pride in thinking he can work things out for himself. Jack will pitch on Wednesday, and I'm pretty sure I'll do a little teaching during his pre-game warmup. I want to present my ideas on how he can shake his slump. Normally, I build confidence and review opposing hitters during this warm-up. Timing is important with Jack. You can forget talking to him if he's not in the right mood. I hope my timing is right on Wednesday.

I also talked to Dan Petry, and told him he would not pitch on Monday unless his stiff shoulder was 100 percent. He told me he was going to pitch, but that his shoulder did not feel 100 percent. Dan has his heart set on leading the league in starts, which is understandable. There's a certain amount of pride a starting pitcher derives from toeing the rubber every fourth or fifth day.

I discussed Dan's situation with Sparky during the game. Sparky decided we would start rookie Roger Mason on Monday if we won today's game. Dan was a little upset. I think he wanted to pitch the pennant clincher, which a Monday victory will be if the Blue Jays lose their game to the Boston Red Sox.

Jack stopped by and asked to be moved up to Tuesday from Wednesday if we don't clinch on Monday. Jack also wants to pitch the clincher. I recognized his ambition, but told him our rotation was set and that we weren't thinking of personal glory. I don't think Sparky would change the playoff rotation of Jack, Dan, and Milt, although circumstances could dictate a switch. Milt has the hot hand. Juan worked five good innings today to win for the ninth time. He is 5-3 in his past ten starts with a 2.98 earned run average. Jack and Dan both have experienced physical problems that are reflected in their statistics. Dan is 3-4 with a 4.68 earned run average in his past ten starts. Jack is 4-4, with a 5.31 ERA.

Willie wanted to work one inning today to sharpen his control. He allowed one run, which is not unusual in lopsided games. Willie has permitted nineteen runs in forty-four and two-thirds innings for a 3.83 earned run average in games decided by four or more runs. Conversely, he has allowed nine runs in eighty-seven innings (0.93 ERA) in games decided by three or fewer runs, and just three runs in fifty-four and two-thirds innings (0.49 ERA) in one-run or two-run victories. This is because he, like most of our relief pitchers, experiments when we are way ahead. It's an excellent opportunity to work on a new pitch, or to add a new wrinkle to your pitching motion. Most pitchers deliberately alter their pattern of pitching when a game is not on the line. Why show a hitter your best stuff when the game is out of reach?

There's one other feature of Hernandez that has contributed to his overwhelming success. His first-batter efficiency is outstanding. Willie has retired the first batter he faced in fifty-eight of his seventy-three appearances, which is a pretty skimpy .205 on-base percentage for those batters. His first-batter efficiency is even better when he enters in the middle of an inning—four of twenty-five have reached for a .160 on-base percentage. Willie's temperament is outstanding for a relief pitcher. He has enormous confidence. We urge relievers to throw their first pitch for a strike and to get that first batter out. After all, this is why the manager summoned them.

That first strike is the most important pitch in baseball. A .350 hitter becomes a .250 hitter if the pitcher gets ahead in

the count because the batter has less of a chance of receiving
the type of pitch he prefers.

TIGERS 8, BLUE JAYS 3   95 – 54

PITCHER	IP	H	R-ER	BB	SO	ERA
Berenguer (9-10)	5.0	3	2-1	3	4	3.60
Scherrer	1.0	0	0-0	0	1	2.38
Lopez	2.0	1	0-0	1	2	2.74
Hernandez	1.0	2	1-1	0	0	1.91

*Whitaker's grand slam on September 17 reduced our
magic number to one*

W E were hoping for an instant replay of the day the Tigers clinched the pennant sixteen years ago. Instead, the ice melted on fifty-four bottles of champagne. Our 7-3 victory over the Milwaukee Brewers sewed up a tie, but the Toronto Blue Jays scored twice in the ninth inning to defeat the Boston Red Sox 5-4 and put our celebration on hold.

Sparky and I have reverted to trickery in order to clinch. We handed Roger Mason the starting assignment tonight, and tomorrow will give the ball to rookie Randy O'Neal. There is a method to our madness. Petry and Morris have not been pitching well, but both are eager to be the starting pitcher in our pennant-clinching victory. Both volunteered for tomorrow's assignment. We have devised our strategy with psychology and the physical well-being of Dan and Jack in mind. Jack will start on Wednesday to allow him four days of rest between starts. Dan will be skipped a turn to permit his stiff shoulder ample time to mend. Their minds, we believe, will be working overtime. I talked to a Detroit reporter about our pitching rotation, while omitting our psychological ploy. I want Jack and Dan to read this in the paper. I feel this will provide them with incentive and help both shake their slumps. As expected, Jack is disappointed, and Dan is upset. I told Dan I enjoyed seeing his feelings a little ruffled. I told him his irritation might help him more mentally than physically. I expect Dan to smoke the New York Yankees on Saturday.

This strategy is part of our grand scheme to determine our pitching rotation for the American League Championship Series. Berenguer and Wilcox both have been pitching better than Dan and Jack over the past month. Sparky and I are inclined to start Jack and Dan in the first two playoff games, but this requires some justification. A good start or two by Dan and Jack would provide that.

Today was hectic, beginning with a lengthy meeting between Sparky, myself, coach Dick Tracewski, general manager

Bill Lajoie, and scouts Rick Ferrell and Hoot Evers. We discussed in detail the Chicago Cubs, who are a potential World Series opponent. The report was compiled by Evers and advance scout Boots Day, and dealt with every Cubs player and every square inch of Wrigley Field. There will be additional reports on the Cubs, as well as the San Diego Padres, in the next couple of weeks.

I was summoned to the office of club president Jim Campbell after our discussion of the Cubs. Jim is a wonderful person for whom I have the utmost respect. He also is capable of skulduggery. "I was watching the game on television the other night and I saw you walk to the mound," Campbell told me. "I said to myself, 'There's another Ralph Houk.' " Houk managed the Tigers for five seasons, retired following the 1978 campaign, but returned to baseball in 1981 as manager of the Red Sox. "Houk wanted to retire and get out of uniform, but he came back," continued Campbell. "I feel you would do the same. I want you to think about your decision to retire and be absolutely certain that's what you want. We want you back." The squeeze is on.

The pre-game clubhouse was chaotic. A television camera supported by a tripod and set on a platform was in place to capture the post-game festivities. A large group of reporters was milling around to chronicle the scene. The clubhouse phone rang incessantly. I even conducted a telephone interview from the dugout with a Durham, North Carolina, radio station.

Roger Mason demonstrated tremendous poise for a rookie pitching a possible pennant-clinching game. He allowed two runs in six innings and left with a 7-2 lead that was preserved by Lopez. I really like Roger's makeup. He goes about his business in workmanlike fashion. He yearns to learn how to pitch effectively, and he has guts. There is definitely a spot for him on this club next season. We're just going to have to move someone out.

Throughout the game, everyone's attention was on the scoreboard. The Blue Jays–Red Sox game was running a little ahead of ours. In our eighth inning, Carolyn, seated adjacent

A few pointers helped Roger Mason drop our magic number to one

to our dugout, advised me the Blue Jays had lost, 4-3. I told Sparky and the word spread down the bench to all the players. There was a lot of hugging and hand-slapping. We felt we had won this division a long time ago, but nothing can replace the actual event. We brought our relief pitchers and bullpen catcher in from the bullpen to spare them from being jostled by enthusiastic fans. The one hitch was that my wife, bless her, had received false information. The scoreboard informed everyone of a Toronto victory, and a hush fell over the crowd of 34,191.

TIGERS 7, BREWERS 3   96 — 54

PITCHER	IP	H	R-ER	BB	SO	ERA
Mason (1-1)	6.0	6	2-2	2	4	3.50
Lopez (S14)	3.0	3	1-1	1	1	2.74

THE first shower of champagne to hit my bald head came simultaneously from Dan Petry and Aurelio Lopez as our clubhouse erupted in carbonation and joy. As a player, I had participated in three World Series victory celebrations. None compared to this shindig, even though we are still one step removed from the World Series. We beat the Milwaukee Brewers 3-0 in a combined shutout by rookie Randy O'Neal and Willie Hernandez.

I never dreamed so many tears and so much champagne would flow on this night. Our championship, in my opinion, had been a foregone conclusion since we swept the Blue Jays in Toronto earlier this month. The players felt the same way, but it didn't prevent them from releasing pent-up emotions that had been building after our fantastic start. Gibson dumped a cooler of water and ice on owner Tom Monaghan. Kirk accidentally conked Sparky on the head with a champagne bottle. Sparky suffered a puncture wound along his scalp and retreated to the trainer's room with blood streaming down his smiling face. Boys will be boys. Rozie and Morris did an abbreviated striptease. Dave began collecting beer cans. "That's ten cents," he said each time he picked up another empty.

The coaches stood in the wings. We had worked very hard for this moment. I hugged John Fetzer, who was sole owner of the Tigers from 1961 to 1983. I congratulated Bill Lajoie on his deals. Think about it! He brought us Willie, Dave Bergman, Rusty Kuntz, Ruppert Jones, Darrell Evans, and Bill Scherrer. Lajoie winked at me and said he had saved the kid pitchers, Roger Mason and O'Neal, for September. "I didn't want to give them all to you at one time," Lajoie joked.

One of the Detroit cops came into the dugout and I traded my baseball hat for his pair of spurs. His souvenir isn't as practical. After all, I do own horses.

The party bubbled on and on. It looks like we finally have overcome the legend of the 1968 World Champion Tigers. The

Willie clinches the division

A night I'll always remember

state of Michigan has been clinging to that team for sixteen years. Tiger fans have felt a close bond with many of the '68 heroes: Mickey Stanley, Mickey Lolich, Willie Horton, Bill Freehan, Al Kaline, Norm Cash, Jim Northrup, and Denny McLain. I've been here five years and all I've heard was how the '68 Tigers did this or did that. They had a great year and they were the World Champions, but I think Sparky, the players, and all of the coaches—even Gates Brown and Dick Tracewski, who played on that team—are tired of the constant reminders and comparisons. We want people to talk about the '84 Tigers.

Jim Northrup is writing a column on our club for the *Detroit Free Press.* This isn't right. Northrup doesn't know a lot about our club. Kaline or Freehan would be more qualified. They helped us in spring training and they travel frequently with us during the season in their capacities as telecasters. They'd give the readers better insight.

After one recent game the television was blaring in our clubhouse and the announcer made reference to the '68 Tigers. One of our players hollered, "The hell with the '68 Tigers. We're the '84 Tigers." As great as the Tigers were in 1968, they are history. Now we're the heroes.

Willie deservedly sealed the championship. He struck out Jim Sundberg at 10:05 P.M. Our celebration had begun a few minutes earlier with some handshakes and back-patting in the dugout. We were grateful for the victory. Clinching on the basis of a Toronto loss would not have made us feel like we did it.

Randy's performance was unbelievable for a kid confronted with that pressure. He allowed only four hits in seven innings and retired the final eleven batters he faced. He is the most heralded rookie pitcher in Detroit since Mark Fidrych.

I must confess that I felt some additional pride in the fact that we won with a shutout. Pitching is the cornerstone of most championship teams. It is the foundation of ours. We could not have prevailed without contributions from each of our pitchers. I salute all of them.

Petry and Morris may have deserved to start this game, but I feel my little hunch to cast them as spectators will pay off

CHRISTOPHER CHAGNON/PHOTOCORE

The team enjoys watching highlights of the game

for us in the playoffs. Dan agreed. He threw before the game and said his arm felt sound. "As always," Dan said, "you were right."

TIGERS 3, BREWERS 0   97 – 54

PITCHER	IP	H	R-ER	BB	SO	ERA
O'Neal (1-0)	7.0	4	0-0	1	6	0.00
Hernandez (S30)	2.0	2	0-0	0	2	1.89

PETRY received a telegram from his father today. Dan shared it with me. It read:

> Dear Son,
> Thanks for making my one and only big decision the right one. I still remember my tears and anguish the summer of '76. They are tears of joy in the fall of '84. I only dreamed that it would come to this. Good luck and enjoy the games and moments to come. Love your mother because she had the wisdom to let us men be free to make the choice.
> Love, Dad

Ronald Petry, like any caring father, had second thoughts about allowing his son to embark on a professional baseball career at the age of seventeen. Dan was selected by the Tigers in the fourth round of the 1976 amateur draft. His father rejected the Tiger contract offer. His mother, Aleene, fretted at the prospect of her son living in a dingy hotel in Bristol, Virginia, which would have been Dan's first professional stop. Mr. Petry tossed and turned the entire night. In the morning, he called the Tigers and accepted their offer. Dan got the opportunity to realize his dream of pitching in the major leagues.

Dan was deeply moved by the telegram. I was impressed by his father's ability to capture the essence of nine years of hard work Dan put into his craft. That telegram will always have a prominent spot in Dan's scrapbook.

Sparky and I have our tentative pitching rotation for the American League Championship Series. Jack will pitch the opener, Dan will go in the second game, and Milt in the third game. If necessary, Jack will pitch the fourth game, and Dan the fifth. This has been our rotation the entire season. We always felt Jack would pitch the opener and that Dan would pitch the second game, but we have to make certain that their arms are completely sound.

Jack won his eighteenth game tonight as we completed

a three-game sweep of the Milwaukee Brewers by handing them a 4-2 setback. This "day after," Sparky flooded the lineup with reserve players. They gave Jack a 4-1 lead after three innings. Jack's control was better—he issued only one walk in his six innings. We set our playoff plan in motion by using Scherrer, Rozema, and Hernandez for one inning each.

I must be concerned with the bullpen as well as my starters so we enter the playoffs at full throttle. Relievers such as Scherrer, Bair, Lopez, and Hernandez require ample work to remain finely tuned.

Sparky held a pre-game meeting with the players. He hopes they maintain a clear perspective. We are the champions, but as he reminded us, the Milwaukee Brewers were league champs in 1982 and two years later they are in last place. And he wanted the team to think about the reigning World Champions. Last year's heroes are battling for a third place finish in the division.

Sparky has tremendous highs and lows. It's just the way he is. If we lose two straight games he's on a downer. He even imagined us losing seven straight games to the Yankees after we had lost our opening game to the Blue Jays during the September 14-16 series in Detroit. He was bugged all season by the thought of losing our lead after the big start. He would not admit we had clinched the championship until it was official and on paper.

Now we are there. Sparky gave the players tips on how to conduct themselves during the post-season frenzy. Telephones will ring without interruption as reporters seek out stories and every friend and relative badgers for tickets. And room service is a must to avoid being mobbed by fans.

Our players were aware of the truths in Sparky's speech. They had been besieged by media and fans all season long. That experience should prove beneficial now.

TIGERS 4, BREWERS 2   98 – 54

PITCHER	IP	H	R-ER	BB	SO	ERA
Morris (18-11)	6.0	9	2-2	1	3	3.76
Scherrer	1.0	1	0-0	0	0	2.19
Rozema	1.0	0	0-0	0	1	3.78
Hernandez (S31)	1.0	2	0-0	0	0	1.87

197

FRIDAY, SEPTEMBER 21   DETROIT

O NE responsibility of Sparky's and of each coach is to
submit scouting reports on every player in the league.
This helps the front office shape its thinking on possible off-
season trades. It's a time-consuming process, but part of my
job description. I try to tackle it diligently.

Players are ranked in several categories, each of which
requires a numerical rating. Those ratings generally run from
one, which is poor, to five, which is average, to eight, which is
excellent. The categories on a pitcher's report include fastball,
curve, control, changeup, slider, poise, overall, and interest (our
interest in possibly acquiring this particular player). The categories request present and future numerical ratings. The report
cards on possible playoff opponents serve a different purpose
now. I graded Mike Witt, a six-foot-four right-handed pitcher for
the California Angels, as low as four for present changeup to
as high as seven for his curveball. The majority of my grades
on Witt were sixes, and I determined we should have a definite
interest in acquiring his services.

The report also calls for comments on each player. On
Witt, I said:

> Has probably one of the best curveballs in the league. Good
> moving fastball. Has fast and slow move to first. You can run
> on him if you observe closely. Has improved every year and
> has fine arm. Has no pickoff moves to second or third base.
> Tires in late innings.

The categories on the hitters sheet include hitting, power,
running, arm strength, arm accuracy, fielding, range, aggressiveness, overall evaluation, and interest. My grades on Gary
Gaetti, the third baseman of the Minnesota Twins, ranged from
a four for running to a seven for aggressiveness. The bulk of
Gaetti's grades were fives and sixes. I expressed a definite interest in acquiring his services should he become available. My
comments read:

Good fastball hitter. High ball and inside type hitter. Pitch down and away. Pull hitter. Play outfield and infield accordingly. Will not bunt, below-average runner. Good competitor who will battle. Has average range defensively and average arm, but very accurate. Looks like leader on club.

We had our five-game winning streak snapped tonight by the New York Yankees. They rallied from a 3-0 deficit to defeat Wilcox, 5-3, and terminate his personal six-game winning streak. The Yankees walked away with this game. Milt issued five bases on balls in five and one-third innings, including one to Butch Wynegar to force home the eventual winning run. Bill Scherrer relieved Milt and walked a second run home. Milt complained of dizziness after his performance, no doubt a result of the previous night's euphoria. Sparky and I have not yet informed Milt, Jack, and Dan of our tentative pitching rotation for the Championship Series. I did rib all three by telling them they each deserved to start so the only solution was to pitch each for three innings in the opener. I sincerely believe that each of the three is worthy of the first-game assignment. We haven't lost more than four consecutive games all season because these three wouldn't allow it. Jack was phenomenal the first two months in winning ten of his first eleven decisions, Dan picked up the slack in June and July by winning seven of nine decisions, and Milt has won nine of eleven decisions since the All-Star break. Thanks, fellas.

YANKEES 5, TIGERS 3   98 – 55

PITCHER	IP	H	R-ER	BB	SO	ERA
Wilcox (17-8)	5.1	5	5-4	5	3	4.05
Scherrer	0.2	0	0-0	1	0	2.08
Bair	1.0	1	0-0	2	0	3.77
Lopez	2.0	0	0-0	0	0	2.70

SATURDAY, SEPTEMBER 22   DETROIT

PETRY dispelled any doubts about the condition of his pitching arm. He tossed a four-hit shutout and struck out nine as we beat the Yankees 6-0.

I guess Dan didn't like his eleven days of rest and all the talk in the papers about him possibly being relegated to starting the third game of the playoffs. He directed his anger toward the Yankees, as I had hoped. He was in control this entire game and that stemmed from his aggressive approach.

Dan was mad at Sparky and me. He said he wanted to show us that he is an outstanding power pitcher, and not the finesse pitcher we've seen recently. He made his point. Jack Morris receives his opportunity tomorrow.

TIGERS 6, YANKEES 0   99 – 55

PITCHER	IP	H	R-ER	BB	SO	ERA
Petry (18-8)	9.0	4	0-0	2	9	3.29

J ACK will pitch the opener on October 2 in the city of the West Division champion, followed by Dan on October 3 and Milt on October 5. We informed each pitcher of our decision. Jack requested a meeting with Sparky and me in Sparky's office. "Listen, I want you both to know that if you start Dan or Milt in the opener I won't be hurt," he said. "I'll go out and pitch the best I possibly can, regardless of which game it is. I realize now that I'm a team man, and don't care only about Jack Morris. I want to win the whole thing. It finally hit me how important this is to the entire organization." I was heartened by Jack's words, especially in view of all the problems this season.

Jack proceeded to pitch two-hit ball for six shutout innings. We beat New York 4-1 in our final home game of the regular season. This was Jack's best outing since the All-Star break. His slider was vastly improved and so was his split-fingered fastball, which had not been effective the past two months. We had devoted a lot of bullpen time to rediscovering its effectiveness. Jack finally solved the problem by gripping the ball a little deeper in his fingers and by exerting more pressure with his thumb upon release. This gave the ball more of a downward rotation.

Scherrer provided one scoreless inning and Hernandez allowed one run over the final two innings. This was Willie's thirty-second save in as many opportunities. He had not pitched for three days and was affected by the layoff. He issued consecutive unintentional walks for the first time this season. I guess we can't expect perfection every time, although we've come to expect that from Willie. He is a legitimate Most Valuable Player candidate.

I really appreciated a remark attributed to Ralph Houk in today's papers. A condescending Boston writer suggested to Houk, who manages the Red Sox, that outfielder Dwight Evans is worthy of MVP consideration. "Are you kidding!" Houk replied. "Anybody who doesn't vote for Willie Hernandez doesn't know anything about baseball."

Don Mattingly and Dave Winfield, Yankee teammates who are battling for the batting championship, today were held hitless in the same game for the first time since August 14. Winfield, in fact, managed only one hit in eleven at-bats this series. He hit seven home runs against us last year and had collected thirteen hits in his first nineteen at-bats against us this year. I believe one reason we controlled Mattingly and Winfield is that both are pressing for the batting title.

Our final home game was a milestone. The victory was our hundredth of the season to move us within four wins of breaking the club record. That, of course, is held by the 1968 Tigers. The victory also stamped Sparky as the only manager to guide two different clubs to one hundred wins. The crowd of 39,198, which pushed our home attendance above the 2,700,000 mark, kept chanting "Sparky," "Sparky" after the game. All the players congregated around the television set in the clubhouse to see their little leader take a bow. Sparky had promised the Tigers a pennant and he delivered. I had retrieved the game ball and each of our players who participated in the game signed it. I presented the trophy to Sparky after his curtain call.

For the first time in my five-year association with the Tigers, the home finale didn't inspire any strains of Auld Lang Syne. We'll be back for an Octoberfest.

TIGERS 4, YANKEES 1   100 – 55

PITCHER	IP	H	R-ER	BB	SO	ERA
Morris (19-11)	6.0	2	0-0	4	4	3.66
Scherrer	1.0	0	0-0	0	0	1.93
Hernandez (S32)	2.0	0	1-1	2	1	1.91

W E watch the scoreboard differently now. No longer are we concerned with the Toronto Blue Jays. Instead, we're keeping close tabs on the West Division. Most of the team believes our playoff opponent will be Kansas City or California.

We arrived here on a balmy Monday and departed on a frigid Wednesday with two victories in three games. With 102 wins, we are on the doorstep of matching the club record for most victories in one season, which is 103. I can't believe it's this late in the season.

Berenguer encountered problems in the first inning of Monday's game. That first inning stalked Juan all season. I made my customary stroll to the mound, but not my customary speech. Juan had his head bowed when I arrived. I said, "Do you miss me so much that you want me to come out and talk to you the first inning of every game?" That cracked the ice. Juan laughed and proceeded to allow one run in five innings to defeat the Milwaukee Brewers 7-3. The victory was Juan's tenth, which represents his career-high. He joined Morris, Petry, Wilcox, and Lopez as double-digit winners.

Lopez is my designated assistant when Juan pitches. Aurelio normally waits until the sixth or seventh inning to go to the bullpen. He had made that trip in the first inning. Sparky and I summoned him to return to the dugout to talk to Juan between innings. I told Aurelio what to say to Juan and Aurelio conveyed the message in Spanish. I told Aurelio to tell Juan not to guide his pitches and to be more aggressive. It worked.

Rozema, Bair, Scherrer, and Lopez worked one inning each as part of our scheme to have all our pitchers prepared for the playoffs. Doug allowed a two-run home run to Robin Yount. Those were the only runs Doug has permitted in his past six appearances. Yount hit a low fastball over the plate. That is his power zone. He likes to extend his arms and you have to pitch him up and in.

Prior to Tuesday's game, the players gathered to divide

shares for post-season bonuses. Any player who has been with the team the entire season automatically receives a full share, which could approach $100,000 for this season's World Series winner. A lot of lobbying occurs in these meetings. The amount of a full share rises if fewer partial shares are voted to players who have spent only a portion of the season with the parent club. I'll never forget the first shares meeting I attended in 1956 as a member of the Brooklyn Dodgers. Carl Furillo was the last person to enter the room. "If they ain't in the room, the hell with 'em!" bellowed Furillo.

The voting in these players-only meetings is never made public. The manager and coaches weren't there, although I think Sparky was invited. Talk gets around, however, and I was glad to hear our players were generous. They voted full shares to at least three teammates who weren't with the ballclub the entire season. Rusty Kuntz, Sid Monge, and Ruppert Jones deserved full shares. I hope they got them. But to me the ring is the most important thing, not the money.

We won Tuesday's game 9-1. Randy O'Neal pitched five shutout innings to run his string of major league zeroes to fifteen innings. Randy definitely enhanced his chance to make our club next spring. Sid Monge was one of four relief pitchers used in this game. Sid had not pitched in over a month, but retired the side in order. I kidded him afterward, saying, "You better get some ice on that arm." Sid laughed. He's really a personable guy and I'm sorry he hasn't received more opportunities to pitch, but Sparky is working the people he intends to use in the Championship Series and World Series.

Aurelio suffered his first loss of the season on Wednesday when the Brewers struck for four runs in the eighth inning to claim a 7-5 victory. The loss was particularly upsetting to Aurelio. Wilcox had pitched the first five innings and stood to win his eighteenth game. Milt and Aurelio are best of friends and Aurelio told Milt after the game he never again wanted to pitch in a game that Milt could win. Milt reassured Aurelio everything was fine, and reminded Lopey of the many victories he has saved for him.

Sparky wanted to remove Aurelio in favor of Hernandez as the inning unfolded. I disagreed. Aurelio has won ten games and saved fourteen others. We don't want this sensitive person depressed heading into post-season play. The end result wasn't any more favorable than his removal would have been. I talked to him after the game and told him he was dipping his elbow upon delivery. This robs a pitcher of full velocity. Aurelio acknowledged the mechanical flaw, but remained a forlorn figure. I've got to keep him pumped up.

Monday, September 24
TIGERS 7, BREWERS 3   101 — 55

PITCHER	IP	H	R-ER	BB	SO	ERA
Berenguer (10-10)	5.0	5	1-1	2	3	3.55
Rozema	1.0	1	0-0	0	0	3.74
Bair	1.0	1	2-2	1	0	3.93
Scherrer	1.0	1	0-0	0	0	1.80
Lopez	1.0	0	0-0	0	0	2.68

Tuesday, September 25
TIGERS 9, BREWERS 1   102 — 55

PITCHER	IP	H	R-ER	BB	SO	ERA
O'Neal (2-0)	5.0	2	0-0	0	3	0.00
Monge	1.0	0	0-0	0	0	3.86
Scherrer	1.0	2	0-0	0	0	1.69
Lopez	1.0	2	1-1	0	1	2.73
Hernandez	1.0	0	0-0	0	0	1.90

Wednesday, September 26
BREWERS 7, TIGERS 5   102 — 56

PITCHER	IP	H	R-ER	BB	SO	ERA
Wilcox	5.0	4	1-1	3	2	4.00
Mason	1.0	3	2-2	0	1	4.26
Scherrer	1.0	2	0-0	0	0	1.59
Lopez (10-1)	1.0	3	4-4	2	0	2.97

I had an intriguing discussion with Petry before tonight's game with the Yankees. Dan bombarded me with questions. Am I being the best possible pitcher? How good can I be? Should I set higher goals? I told Dan he has improved every year he's been in the majors, but that he should aspire to win 22-24 games.

Dan also asked if he should pitch any differently in the playoffs and World Series than he has during the regular season. The question shot me back to 1955 when a reporter asked Brooklyn Dodgers manager Walter Alston why he would start a rookie pitcher named Roger Craig in the fifth game of the World Series. "Because I know he's not afraid," responded Alston. I related that story to Dan and told him not to spend time worrying over his start in the second game of the league Championship Series. The electricity will be obvious. The adrenaline is going to flow. Pitch hard and compete hard, and no one will be disappointed in your performance, I advised.

Morris did that tonight in our 2-1 loss to New York. Jack is ready to open the playoffs next Tuesday after limiting the Yankees to one run and two hits in seven innings. He was bidding for his twentieth victory, but left with the game tied at 1-1. Jack was disappointed, but not annoyed. Sparky and I allowed him to pitch one more inning than we had planned in an attempt to get him the twentieth. The main objective, however, is to have Jack prepared for Tuesday. Another inning or two of work might have been too much of a drain. He had already thrown 113 pitches. He sensed a no-hitter—his command was that great—and carried one into the sixth inning. We'll settle for a similar performance on Tuesday.

Jack won't be facing the California Angels. They were eliminated from the West Division race. The Kansas City Royals have a two-game lead over the Minnesota Twins with three games to play. Kansas City, here we come.

Willie suffered this loss on an infield single by Bobby Meacham, a throwing error by rookie shortstop Doug Baker, and a broken bat single by Don Baylor. Willie's three losses have resulted from two broken bat singles and a routine fly that eluded Ruppert Jones, who was cheating by playing extremely shallow in left field. That's how good Willie has been this season.

Wilcox was scheduled to start the season finale here Sunday, but won't. Milt has a little pain in his pitching shoulder. He considered returning to Detroit for another cortisone shot until a Yankee team physician deemed an injection unnecessary. Milt should be able to start next Friday in Detroit. He will test the arm on Tuesday prior to the playoff opener.

My plan for retirement is meeting with resistance. One or two clubs have sent out feelers for my services. Sparky told me a National League team had asked him for a recommendation, and that if I consented he would submit my name. I discussed this possibility with my wife. She will accede to my wishes if I choose to give managing a second fling.

YANKEES 2, TIGERS 1   102 – 57

PITCHER	IP	H	R-ER	BB	SO	ERA
Morris	7.0	2	1-1	6	3	3.60
Hernandez (9-3)	1.0	2	1-1	1	0	1.95

FRIDAY, SEPTEMBER 28   NEW YORK

T HE string of thirty-two consecutive successful save opportunities by Hernandez was broken here tonight by an unwitting pitching coach and manager. Willie inherited a 2-1 lead and runners on first and third with one out in the eighth inning. He retired both the batters he faced, but allowed the tying run to score on a sacrifice fly. Sparky and I didn't even realize what was happening until third base coach Alex Grammas asked me if Willie had inherited a save situation. I wish Alex had not asked. I told Sparky. "If I had known that, I wouldn't have brought in Willie," Sparky responded. Willie understood the situation better than the rest of us. We brought him in because we wanted to win the game, and he afforded us the best chance.

We did win, 4-2, in twelve innings. Bair pitched four hitless innings and Lou Whitaker delivered a two-run home run. Petry started and pitched six sharp innings. He allowed five hits and one run. Dan seems ready to face the Royals, who clinched the West Division championship with a 6-5 conquest of the Oakland A's after Minnesota had squandered a ten-run lead in losing to Cleveland, 11-10.

Our victory was the 103rd of the season, which matches the club record. I reminded Sparky that we had joined company with the '68 Tigers. He cast a whimsical look in my direction and said, "I'll win 'em, big boy, you just count 'em."

TIGERS 4, YANKEES 2 *(12 innings)*   103 – 57

PITCHER	IP	H	R-ER	BB	SO	ERA
Petry	6.0	5	1-1	1	4	3.24
Scherrer	1.0	1	1-1	0	2	2.00
Lopez	0.1	1	0-0	0	0	2.96
Hernandez	0.2	0	0-0	0	0	1.94
Bair (5-3)	4.0	0	0-0	2	2	3.76

I spent this morning plotting how Jack can best beat the Royals when he opens the American League Championship Series on Tuesday in Kansas City. Here's the game plan:

Willie Wilson—Cannot handle the good inside fastball. For some inexplicable reason, that is a trait of most switch-hitters. Wilson is a high-ball hitter and Jack must keep the ball down. Wilson also is their biggest offensive weapon because of his speed. Jack has to keep him off base, which means it's important to get ahead in the count. We don't want to walk this guy.

Pat Sheridan—He has given us trouble this season. Jack must jam him inside.

George Brett—The only pattern to this guy is the fact he's a situation hitter. We won't pitch him inside if the Royals require a home run because Brett will be looking for a pitch to pull. On the other hand, if the situation warrants a single we'll come in on him because he'll be concentrating on making contact. We're better off pitching him away most of the time.

Jorge Orta—Jack has had problems with Orta. He's a low fastball hitter. Jack has to crowd him more.

Frank White—Likes the fastball high and inside. Jack will stay away with sliders, fastballs, and split-fingered fastballs.

Steve Balboni—A high-fastball hitter. Crowd him and keep the pitch low. He thrives on cripple pitches, especially the high breaking ball.

Onix Concepcion—Has more power than most people suspect. Jack must stay down and away.

Don Slaught—Their most prominent hit and run weapon. Come inside and keep the pitches down.

Darryl Motley—Jumps on the fastball up in the strike zone. If Jack keeps his pitches low and away he won't get hurt.

John Wathan—Fights off inside pitches extremely well. Likes the ball up either inside or outside. Jack wants to stay low and away.

We will review this approach prior to Tuesday's game.

We stylishly won our 104th game of the season here today by whipping the New York Yankees 11-3. We are the winningest team in Tiger history. This seems like the year of the Tiger, but a new season begins Tuesday. No one seemed excited about establishing a club record for victories. We are not playing for records. Our goal is to win the World Series, otherwise our record-shattering season will be a bit shallow.

We have won sixteen of our past twenty-two games and are 17-9 in September, during which the team earned run average is 2.83. My staff has allowed only one home run in the past nine games. Pitching is the most vital element in baseball. Pitch well and you establish control. We expect to be in control.

Berenguer won this game by allowing only two hits over six innings. Juan is now 11-10 and has won six of his past eight decisions. However, we do not plan on starting him in either the playoffs or the World Series. This is not a bad reflection on Juan. Jack, Dan, and Milt are more experienced and more capable. Juan is number four in a three-man starting rotation. He understands this is not the time for apologies.

TIGERS 11, YANKEES 3   104 – 57

PITCHER	IP	H	R-ER	BB	SO	ERA
Berenguer (11-10)	6.0	2	1-1	6	1	3.48
Mason (S1)	3.0	3	2-2	3	1	4.50

MIKE Witt of the California Angels pitched a perfect game today against the Texas Rangers. I guess I graded Witt too low.

We were thrashed by the New York Yankees, 9-2, but we're on our way to Kansas City for the playoffs while the Yankees have gone home for a long winter's nap.

Our 35-5 start won this division for us and set the stage for a phenomenal season. We buried everybody at the start and then were able to rise to the occasion when warranted. I feel we have the type of club destined to win the World Series. We just seem to be able to win at will when necessary. There's an old saying every spring: you automatically accept sixty-two defeats, which means you can't expect to win more than a hundred games. Well, one hundred wins is a helluva year. We had a better one.

Jack Morris's no-hitter on national television on April 7 sticks out in my mind. So does Willie Hernandez. I have never seen a pitcher have a better season. Willie deserves to win both the MVP award and the Cy Young award. I've had Cy Young winners before—Randy Jones and Gaylord Perry—but Willie's year was better than either of theirs was.

The mood of our team entering the league Championship Series is upbeat. Dan Petry is wearing a tie embroidered with Old English D's. Jack begged to take a batting practice swing prior to today's game. "Just one swing to prepare for next year's World Series," joked Morris, mindful that there won't be a designated hitter in the 1985 World Series. Gibson told him to get in the outfield where he belonged.

There was some drama to today's game as Yankee teammates Don Mattingly and Dave Winfield went to their final at-bats to determine the league batting championship. Some of the players in our dugout had pencils and paper and were working the batting averages after every at-bat. Winfield seemed to be affected by the pressure. Mattingly, who collected four hits to win the battle by three points, was more loose. There is no disgrace finishing second, however, when your batting average is .340.

Rookie Randy O'Neal started for us and lost the game and his scoreless string of innings. Randy fell victim to the problem that periodically afflicts every pitcher. He had his pitches up in the strike zone and allowed seven runs in three and two-thirds innings.

The regular season is behind us. We are to fly to Kansas City to meet the Royals. It doesn't seem quite fair that we should have to beat the Royals in a five-game series after winning twenty more games than they did during the regular season. But we'll play by the rules and see either the Chicago Cubs or the San Diego Padres in the World Series.

YANKEES 9, TIGERS 2   104 – 58

PITCHER	IP	H	R-ER	BB	SO	ERA
O'Neal (2-1)	3.2	9	7-7	4	1	3.37
Bair	0.1	0	0-0	0	1	3.75
Monge	1.0	2	2-2	1	0	4.00
Lopez	1.0	1	0-0	0	0	2.94
Scherrer	1.0	1	0-0	0	1	1.89
Hernandez	1.0	1	0-0	0	1	1.92

FINAL PITCHING STATISTICS – 1984

NAME	Won	Lost	ERA	G	GS	CG	SHO	Saves	IP	Hits	HR	BB	SO
Abbott	3	4	5.93	13	8	1	0	0	44.0	62	9	8	7
Bair	5	3	3.75	47	1	0	0	4	93.2	82	10	36	57
Berenguer	11	10	3.48	31	27	2	1	0	168.1	146	14	79	118
Hernandez	9	3	1.92	80	0	0	0	32	140.1	96	6	36	113
Lopez	10	1	2.94	71	0	0	0	14	137.2	109	16	52	94
Mason	1	1	4.50	4	2	0	0	1	22.0	23	1	10	15
Monge	1	0	4.00	19	0	0	0	0	36.0	40	5	12	19
Morris	19	11	3.60	35	35	9	1	0	240.1	221	20	87	150
O'Neal	2	1	3.37	4	3	0	0	0	18.2	14	0	6	12
Petry	18	8	3.24	35	35	7	2	0	233.1	231	21	66	144
Rozema	7	6	3.74	29	16	0	0	0	101.0	110	13	18	48
Scherrer	1	0	1.89	18	0	0	0	0	19.0	14	1	8	16
Wilcox	17	8	4.00	33	33	0	0	0	193.2	183	13	66	119
Willis	0	2	7.31	10	2	0	0	0	16.0	25	1	5	5
Team	104	58	3.49	430	162	19	8	51	1464.0	1358	130	489	914

KEY: ERA—earned run average; G—games; GS—games started; CG—complete games; SHO—shutouts; IP—innings pitched; HR—home runs; BB—bases on balls; SO—strikeouts.

Allow me to be brash. I think we'll sweep the Royals in three games.

A lot of media people here see things differently. The stories in today's papers suggest we were just another club except for our phenomenal 35-5 start; they say we coasted to our divisional title and that we weren't exposed to pressure. Some articles claim we are bored by winning, the implication being that we aren't prepared for the league Championship Series.

I disagree. I've never seen a club more determined to win. We've worked very hard to reach this plateau and cleared several obstacles along the way: No other team had to worry about the embarrassment of failing after an unprecedented start. No other team had to cope with the crush of national media attention we received in May and June. No other team was chased by every other team in its league for the entire season. And no other team had to conquer the American League East Division, the one I consider the toughest in baseball. We have a great deal of respect for the Royals. They are good, but we have an outstanding club, one of the best I've seen in my thirty-five years in pro ball. We are deep in every department, including confidence and attitude.

We held a ninety-minute workout this afternoon. There were so many reporters around that I didn't even have a chance to talk to Sparky. The hype is building. Many wives, including mine, are here to share this moment—they had to pay their own way, though. Some clubs foot that bill for the league Championship Series, but not the Tigers. The organization will pay the transportation costs of wives if we make it to the World Series, however. Wives are an important part of post-season events. They offer encouragement and support—and incentive, because they've already spent enough money shopping to devour our championship earnings. These playoffs bring on strong memories—and hopes—for Carolyn, who vividly recalls the treatment we received in 1955 when the Dodgers won the

World Series. Brooklyn embraced its Dodgers; Detroit will do the same for its Tigers.

I have great confidence in Jack. He has had his ups and downs, but he's a true champion. I think he'll take command tomorrow night.

W E exploded a lot of myths tonight by whipping the Royals, 8-1, in the opening game of the league Championship Series. Many people felt we would be sabotaged by our relative inexperience in post-season play: none of our starters, and in all only four of our players—Willie Hernandez, Doug Bair, Dave Bergman, and Milt Wilcox—have any playoff experience.

Enthusiasm and determination are great equalizers.

Our pitching dominated tonight. Jack and Willie combined to limit the Royals to only five hits, while Alan Trammell, Larry Herndon, and Lance Parrish each smacked a home run to power our offense. Kirk Gibson made all those fungoes I've hit to him worthwhile by spearing a line drive off the bat of George Brett with two outs and the bases loaded in the third.

I could tell that Morris would have a good game by the way he warmed up in the bullpen. He looked at me with a sinister smile and said, "I've got it tonight; they're not going to hit me." Jack can rise to the occasion better than any pitcher on my staff. His fastball rose accordingly tonight. He was clocked at ninety-seven miles per hour. That's rushing the ball!

He succeeded in our game plan by containing Willie Wilson and Brett, the two biggest weapons in the Royals' attack. Wilson had one harmless single in four at-bats while Brett didn't have any hits at all. Our strategy was to keep Wilson off the basepaths by feeding him a steady diet of inside fastballs. This pitching pattern worked successfully for the Philadelphia Phillies in the 1980 World Series when Wilson managed only four hits in twenty-six at-bats, while striking out twelve times. If Wilson is kept off the bases, Brett is much less of a threat. One reason is that Wilson's base-stealing abilities force a pitcher to throw more fastballs to Brett than he would otherwise. This situation causes a lot of extra pressure for a pitcher, who has a tendency to strive for the perfect pitch. This quest for perfection frequently results in a mistake. In a bases-empty situation, *we* choose how to pitch Brett and we can limit the damage. He will go for the long ball because a single isn't as likely to set off a big inning. We should have good success under these circumstances by pitching him away.

I don't talk to Jack much during his bullpen warm-ups because he is so deep in concentration, but I did ask him to concentrate on getting ahead in the ball-strike count, especially with Wilson. He followed my advice and issued only one walk in seven innings before being removed with a blister on the middle finger of his pitching hand. The injury isn't serious and he'll be able to start Game 4 on Saturday in Detroit, if necessary.

Hernandez sealed the victory in decisive fashion. He retired six consecutive batters on a total of sixteen pitches, thirteen of which were strikes. He popped his fastball much better than he had in his previous two outings.

This was a very business-like performance by the whole team. We were prepared and we executed. There was not much cheering or hollering afterward in the clubhouse. This attitude was an extension of our season-long demeanor. We expect to win. We came here to do a job, and tonight we did just that.

There was some concern about the umpiring in this series. The Major League Umpires Association is on strike and both league championships are being worked by amateur umpires. Sparky talked about the strike in a brief pre-game meeting. He urged the players not to question calls because that might apply pressure which could adversely affect a subsequent decision. We got a break when the American League contracted the services of former major-league umpire Bill Deegan. Deegan, who worked behind the plate, did an outstanding job and showed consistency with his strike zone. That is critical to a pitcher. You have to be sure about the umpire's strike zone and you can't allow your pattern of pitching to be disrupted.

TIGERS 8, ROYALS 1   1 — 0

PITCHER	IP	H	R-ER	BB	SO	ERA
Morris (1-0)	7.0	5	1-1	1	4	1.29
Hernandez	2.0	0	0-0	0	2	0.00

WE'VE had a lot of outstanding games this magical season, but none was steeped in as much suspense as this one. We defeated the Royals tonight, 5-3, in a spellbinding eleven-inning game.

John Grubb, one of the most personable guys on the club, delivered a game-winning double off Kansas City relief ace Dan Quisenberry, and Lopez demonstrated how he responds to pressure by pitching three scoreless innings in relief of Petry for the victory. Gibson continued to enhance his position as our dugout leader when Ruppert Jones fouled off a pitch in a bunt situation in the eleventh inning. "Get the damn bunt down," screamed Gibby. "You've got to get the runners over. You've got to do it!" The players looked at Gibson in admiration. Sparky and I smiled at each other.

There is a fierce competitive fire on this club. Dan was the torch. He had the same attitude warming up in the bullpen that Jack had before the first game. "You know, I feel great," Dan told me. "We won last night and they haven't seen our best pitcher yet." I told him he was right. I always try to make my pitchers feel they're the best on their night. This kind of positive thinking can be a powerful force. Tonight it was. I rank Dan's performance the best of his career. He went right at the Royals with an outstanding fastball and slider, and left the game with a 3-2 lead after seven innings.

We called upon Hernandez for the eighth inning. This may have been a mistake on my part. Willie wasn't feeling well; he had a touch of the flu and a sore throat. He warmed up though and said he felt fine. Sparky decided to use him and I agreed. The Royals tied the game on a one-out double by pinch-hitter Hal McRae.

This was a bit annoying to me. I had gone to the mound when McRae was announced as the pinch-hitter, and I told Willie and Lance that McRae would be sitting on a fastball in this situation. I told them to throw him a lot of breaking balls, beginning with a screwball. "Keep it down and away, because he'll be trying to pull the pitch out of the park," were my final words to Willie and Lance. Then I returned to the dugout and watched Willie throw a curve that McRae lashed into the left field corner. I told myself that I wouldn't confront Willie about the pitch if we lost, but would if we won.

"What did you throw McRae?" I asked Willie after the game. "Curve," he responded. "I thought I told you to start him off with the screwball," I said. "Well . . . it was a breaking ball," he protested. I gave him a short lecture on the difference between the curve and the screwball, a distinction Willie was well aware of. I guess Willie and Lance decided on the curve after I left the mound. Sparky and I want the pitchers to throw what we decide. We'll take the blame under those circumstances.

Lopez took over in the ninth inning and walked Willie Wilson with two outs. This is precisely what we didn't want to happen. Wilson represented the winning run, so I went to work on rubbing him out. I signalled for Aurelio to throw to first base several times. No tipoff from Wilson. Aurelio threw one strike to the batter, Lynn Jones, and I then decided to pitch out twice in a row. Wilson went on the first pitchout, and Lance threw him out easily. This was only the second time in thirty-nine attempts this season that Wilson has been thrown out stealing with a right-handed pitcher on the mound. A pitchout call is worthless unless the execution is nearly perfect. Aurelio threw to the right spot—chest high and eighteen inches outside. Lance stepped out, set up, and threw in one fluid motion. A nice play all around.

Jack came to me after the game and said the pitchout was the turning point. We grinned at each other as occasional combatants and long-time friends.

We took a bus from Royals Stadium to the Kansas City airport for our flight to Detroit. I told Jim Campbell that I had received a call from the policeman who swapped his spurs for my cap when we clinched the divisional championship. The policeman told me he'd give me his saddle if we won the league championship and his horse if we won the World Series. Jim laughed. I wouldn't mind another horse in my stable.

We arrived at Detroit's Metropolitan Airport at 4 A.M. Thursday. The plane had to be diverted to another terminal because of the thousands of people waiting to greet us. And when our bus reached Tiger Stadium, at least a thousand people were waiting for us. I was flabbergasted at this demonstration of support. The fans deserve what we're going to give them—the World Championship.

The media learned on Wednesday of my intention to retire. Ernie Harwell interviewed me on his pre-game show and the print reporters swarmed on me like bees. In late July, I was 100 percent certain of retiring. Now I'm only 90 percent certain. I'll worry about retirement later.

The players were not reluctant to express opinions on my possible retirement. Jack was surprisingly outspoken. "I think the key is how Roger handles Sparky," Jack told reporters. "Rog is like a second opinion during the game. If Sparky has any doubts, he talks to Rog and they make a decision. They have that kind of rapport. Rog does more than what is expected of a pitching coach. I'll miss him."

When he was asked about my public criticism of his behavior, Jack said, "I didn't appreciate it at all, but I think Rog had a little motivation in mind. It may have worked. That was just one time Rog didn't handle himself in his normal manner. I don't think he meant it directly. Deep down I think Rog believes in me, and deep down we both have a lot of pride. We're both a lot alike so there's bound to be some friction."

Aurelio was perhaps the most touching. "Roger is one of the best guys I've met in my life. He's a gentleman. He knows how to control pitchers. He always listens and always tries to help. I've never met another person in baseball like him. I think baseball is losing a big man."

Lance too paid me a very high compliment that I will treasure always: "If I ever was a manager, I'd pick Roger Craig as my pitching coach. He has the right attitude. He's done a remarkable job with this staff, and he's one guy who deserves a lot of credit for us being in the league Championship Series."

Milt recognized how strongly I feel about positive thinking. "He doesn't let one or two bad outings upset him. Sparky used to, and the pitcher would be dumped from the starting rotation. Rog realizes pitchers have slumps just like hitters. Do you sit Lance on the bench if he goes into a slump for a couple of days?"

"The staff loves Rog," said Marty Castillo. "The staff is comfortable with him. He's positive at times Sparky can't be positive. I've never seen him come to the mound and say anything negative. Rog is always picking guys up with his encouragement. He also takes pressure off the catcher. If a batter has a 2-2 count and has fouled off five pitches, I might be baffled. I'll look to Rog in the dugout and ask him to call the pitch. He won't retire. He wouldn't leave me."

Marty always has had a sense of humor.

"We'll stay in touch if Rog does retire," said Dan. "I won't hesitate to call him if I run into problems. I'll tell him to get down to Anaheim Stadium when we're in town. Roger builds confidence. There was no doubt in my mind that I would succeed in the major leagues after my first day of spring training with Rog."

I'm going to make certain that Dan has my telephone number.

TIGERS 5, ROYALS 3 *(11 innings)*   2 − 0

PITCHER	IP	H	R-ER	BB	SO	ERA
Petry	7.0	4	2-2	1	4	2.57
Hernandez	1.0	2	1-1	1	1	3.00
Lopez (1-0)	3.0	4	0-0	1	2	0.00

Y OU can't beat modern technology. I'm at my condominium
on this off-day watching tapes of our first two victories over
the Kansas City Royals.

Retire? We'll wait and see.

My mind is on the National League where the Chicago
Cubs can clinch the pennant by defeating the San Diego Padres
tonight in San Diego. I'm pulling for the Padres—it would be
nice to be near my home for the World Series. My family and
a lot of friends would be able to attend the games.

I have not set foot in Jack Murphy Stadium since I was
fired as manager of the Padres following the 1979 season.
Although I was disappointed to have to leave San Diego, I
harbor no grudges. I'm happy and proud of the Padres' accomplishments this season.

I spent much of today going over scouting reports on the
Cubs submitted by Boots Day, Hoot Evers, Rick Ferrell, and
Frank Skaff. Those guys have spent ten days to two weeks
studying the Cubs and searching for patterns that could help
us win the World Series. Jim Frey, the Chicago manager, usually plays by the book: he rarely gambles. However, he will not
hesitate to run Bob Dernier and Ryne Sandberg in close games.
Dernier and Sandberg are the Cubs' best basestealers. Dernier,
especially, will attempt a steal at any time, regardless of the
ball-strike count on the batter or the number of outs. He will
also bunt with two strikes and steal on three-ball, no-strike
pitches.

I think the Cubs are a very good paper match for us. Their
offensive strength is primarily right-handed. Our starting pitching is all right-handed. Our offensive strength is better left-
handed. Their only left-handed pitcher is Steve Trout. Our
pitching and defense is superior. So is our team speed.

Rick Sutcliffe, who came to the Cubs from the Cleveland
Indians in June and proceeded to win sixteen of seventeen
decisions, is their pitching ace. We know Sutcliffe well and have

a 2-2 record against him while scoring twenty-five runs in thirty-five innings. We can run on him. He has a high leg kick and a slow release time from the moment he breaks from the set position to delivery of the pitch. He frequently throws breaking pitches when behind and generally starts batters off with his fastball. We have to make him throw his curveball for strikes. He records a lot of strikeouts on curves out of the strike zone. His chief weapons, however, are his slider and fastball. We'll be looking to hit a lot of those first-pitch fastballs. Sutcliffe has an unorthodox pickoff move to second base: he turns in the direction of third base to start his move. The great majority of pitchers pivot toward first base.

Relief pitcher George Frazier is familiar to us, too. Frazier spent time in the American League with the Yankees and the Indians. He throws a spitball, which we'll bring to the attention of the home plate umpire in an attempt to discourage him from throwing it.

Here's a sketch of their key players:

Bob Dernier—Stands close to the plate. Jam him with fastballs and throw him a steady diet of breaking pitches. Keep him off the bases! He gets a good jump and makes things happen, much like Willie Wilson. Tries to pull everything. Hits a lot of ground balls to third base. A good outfielder with an average arm.

Ryne Sandberg—Tough to pattern. Has good power and uses the whole field. Cubs' most consistent player. Has great speed. Keep the ball down and throw him mostly curves and sliders on the outside part of the plate.

Gary Matthews—Good power. Doesn't like off-speed pitches. Will chase high fastballs. Throw him curves and sliders away and then bust him inside with fastballs. Make sure the fastballs are off the plate because he stands far off the plate. Can steal a base when least expected. A bad outfielder. Cannot throw. Take an extra base if the ball is hit to his left.

Leon Durham—Fastballs low and away are his bread and butter. Throw the fastball up and away. Mix in off-speed stuff and fastballs up and in. He has trouble getting the head of his bat out in front of good inside fastballs. Runs well for his size. Will steal second and third base. Average fielder with average arm.

Keith Moreland —Presently in a slump. Loves hanging pitches inside. Change speeds and location because he uses entire field. Always hits to right field with two strikes. He can't run and has no range in the outfield.

Ron Cey —Serve up mostly breaking pitches low and away. He tries to pull everything. Can use straight changeup with success. Frequently swings at 3-0 pitches, as do other Cubs, especially if the wind is blowing out at Wrigley Field. You can bunt on him at third.

Jody Davis —High fastball hitter. Keep breaking pitches low and away. Doesn't run well and is good double-play candidate. His power is to left-center field. Strong arm with quick release, but sometimes erratic. Also can be lazy on blocking balls in dirt.

Morris should fare well against this club because of his good fastball and the ability to throw the split-fingered fastball and straight changeup. Wilcox also seems to match up well with the Cubs. Milt changes speeds very effectively. Petry's off-speed pitches aren't quite as good as Jack's or Milt's. Dan's fastball and slider must be extremely sharp.

Ed Whitson, of the Padres, proved our scouts correct. He shackled the Cubs with breaking pitches low and away in San Diego's 7-1 victory tonight in San Diego. I may yet have to pull out that Padres report.

MY prediction came true. We swept the Kansas City Royals in three games. We're in the World Series!

I've never been more proud of my staff. Our meal ticket to the World Series was pitching. Pitchers and pitching coaches dream of nights like tonight. Imagine—defeating the Royals 1-0! I still can't believe it!

Any 1-0 victory, whether it's in the major leagues or in the minors, is a gutty performance—but Milt's effort in a championship game was spectacular. We provided him with a one-run lead in the second inning when Marty Castillo beat a dou-

Milt established his curve and split-fingered fastball in Game 3

ble play on sheer hustle as Chet Lemon scored. Milt then took charge. The key to his game was his hybrid curve, sort of a cross between a curve and slider. He was unable to establish the pitch in the first two innings, but between innings I encouraged him not to foresake it. He didn't, and it accounted for most of his eight strikeouts. Milt is the only pitcher to have won championship-clinching games in both leagues. (His first was for Sparky's Reds in the 1970 National League series.) He also tied a playoff record by striking out four consecutive batters—Jorge Orta, Darryl Motley, Steve Balboni, and Frank White, spread over the fourth and fifth innings. Only four pitchers have accomplished that feat. Milt's done it twice: in 1970 he mowed down Matty Alou, Fred Patek, Roberto Clemente, and Willie Stargell as a hard-throwing twenty-year-old. The eight strikeouts also matched his season-high. There's no question this was Milt's best performance of the season.

I believe that Jack, Dan, and Milt all saved their best performances for the playoffs. Morris and Petry each pitched seven strong innings in the first two games. Milt was at least their equal. The Royals wound up with only three hits, all singles, and failed to advance any runner beyond first base.

Sparky and I were tempted to let Milt try for his first complete game of the season. After eight innings, I asked him how he felt. "Great," he replied. I asked him if he wanted to pitch the ninth, and he said he did, but then he reminded me that the Royals had three left-handed batters scheduled to hit. Willie, Milt said unselfishly, was the man for the job. He was right. Willie worked the ninth inning and allowed only a two-out infield single to Hal McRae. We are an incredible 94-0 this season when leading in the ninth inning.

The Royals wound up with only three hits, all singles, and failed to advance any runner beyond first base. They had managed only four runs and eighteen hits in twenty-nine innings. That's a microscopic earned run average of 1.27 for my staff. Kansas City also failed to steal a base in two attempts. I'll claim partial credit for that and tip my hat to Parrish, who did a masterful job of handling the staff the entire series.

Tom Brookens gives me a hug after we swept the American League title

Jack Morris and a teammate douse each other with champagne

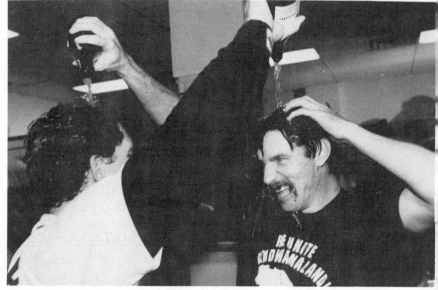

"They shut us down," said Royals manager Dick Howser. "They deserve a lot of credit to have led the league in earned run average pitching in Tiger Stadium. That's almost like leading the league in ERA at Fenway Park."

"The maturity of the pitchers and Lance Parrish is the

biggest change," said Bill Deegan, the fill-in umpire who worked all three games behind the plate. "I saw them during my final season before retiring in 1980. They were throwers and not pitchers. Now, they throw with their heads instead of their arms."

That's my reward for five years of hard work.

The post-game celebration was not as raucous as our East Division party. This was more of an emotional relief. I continually fought back tears. All my pitchers poured champagne over me and said they wouldn't let me retire. I was deeply touched, especially by Mr. Lopez. Aurelio hugged me and said, "You can't retire. You're my man. If you retire, I will retire." Muchas gracias, Señor Smoke.

Jim Campbell called me early in the day and asked me to stop by his office before the game. Bill Lajoie was present, also. I was offered a two-year contract that would make me the highest-paid pitching coach in baseball. Even before I looked at the contract, I told them I'm still leaning toward retirement. I gave them no idea when to expect my decision. The offer is very generous. I will give it serious consideration, but the World Series is foremost on my mind right now.

Meanwhile, the Cubs still have not scored their third victory over the Padres, but they lead the series two games to one. We are off tomorrow and I intend to watch the game on television to pick up some pointers.

TIGERS 1, ROYALS 0   3 – 0

PITCHER	IP	H	R-ER	BB	SO	ERA
Wilcox (1-0)	8.0	2	0-0	2	8	0.00
Hernandez (S1)	1.0	1	0-0	0	0	2.25

LEAGUE CHAMPIONSHIP SERIES STATISTICS

PITCHER	G	GS	W-L	Saves	IP	H	R-ER	ERA	BB	SO
Morris	1	1	1-0	0	7.0	5	1-1	1.29	1	4
Hernandez	3	0	0-0	1	4.0	3	1-1	2.25	1	3
Petry	1	1	0-0	0	7.0	4	2-2	2.57	1	4
Lopez	1	0	1-0	0	3.0	4	0-0	0.00	1	2
Wilcox	1	1	1-0	0	8.0	2	0-0	0.00	2	8
Totals	7	3	3-0	1	29.0	18	4-4	1.27	6	21

I made one promise to the people of San Diego when I was manager of the Padres: I vowed to bring a World Series to town. Well, here I come!

Last night, I watched the Cubs and Padres on television, but I fell asleep on the couch before the game was over. Carolyn woke me and told me the Padres had won to even the series at two games each. This evening I watched and rooted for the Padres in their final game against the Cubs. A Chicago victory meant we would open the World Series here on Tuesday. A San Diego victory meant we would pack in a hurry and get on a charter flight tonight. We packed in a hurry.

I'm excited about going home to San Diego, as my four children will see us in the World Series. I'm also happy for the city and for the Padres. This is only the second year they've finished above .500 in their sixteen-year history. The first was 1978, when I was the manager and we won eighty-four games. I was fired following the 1979 season. Sparky always tells me he predicted it. He wasn't managing when the '79 season began. The Cincinnati Reds had fired him the previous season, and he was at his home in Thousand Oaks, California. He was watering the lawn one day during spring training when he claims he ran into his home and told his wife, Carol, that I would be fired. "Roger Craig just got fired," Sparky maintains he told Carol. She didn't understand. "They just said on a pregame show that the Padres should challenge for the divisional title. No way! Roger made a big mistake last season by winning more games than he had a right to win."

I pored over our scouting reports on the Padres during the course of our four-hour flight west. I don't believe we're going to have much of a problem. They'll throw a lot of left-handed hitters at us, but the split-fingered fastball should be a great equalizer. They do have outstanding speed in Alan Wiggins and Tony Gwynn, both of whom have a tendency to attempt steals on the first or second pitches. We'll just throw to first a lot if they get on base and pitch out on those first or second pitches. I'll be ready and Lance will be ready. I think we can stop them.

Wiggins—A contact hitter. He only grounded into two double plays in nearly 600 at-bats. We'll have to play the corners of the infield close because he likes to bunt and drag bunt.

Gwynn—Another contact hitter with no power. He drives fastballs to the opposite (left) field and pulls off-speed pitches. We intend to jam him with fastballs and sliders, and play him shallow in left field and center field.

Steve Garvey—A tough out when a game is on the line. This could dictate any possible intentional walk strategy. Garvey frequently hits to the opposite (right) field. We'll give him the left field line and pitch him down. He's very selective until he has two strikes. Then he has a tendency to chase bad pitches.

Graig Nettles—San Diego's biggest home run threat. He always gears for the fastball. We can jam him and throw sliders down and in. I think he's a better high-fastball hitter than low-fastball hitter. But he can't run well.

Terry Kennedy—Pulls with power, but looks bad on off-speed pitches and breaking pitches. He doesn't handle pitches away very well. Offensively, we're going to run on Mr. Kennedy. He's a good receiver for a catcher, but hurries his throws. His arm strength is average and his accuracy is below average.

Carmelo Martinez—Has a good knowledge of the strike zone, but pulls most pitches in an attempt to hit home runs. We'll bunch him in the outfield and infield. He's slow out of the batter's box. A good double-play candidate.

Garry Templeton—Has an abundance of talent and is a threat to steal either second or third base. We'll pitch him down and tight, just as we did Willie Wilson, who managed only two singles in thirteen at-bats in the league Championship Series.

We arrived in San Diego at 11 P.M., local time, and 2 A.M. Monday, body time. I have to be up in a few hours to appear on *Good Morning America* with David Hartman and Jim Kaat. Good night, America.

THIS old country boy from Durham, North Carolina, has come a long way from catching fly balls outside his boyhood park. A local ABC-TV affiliate sent a stretch limousine to take Carolyn and me to a studio for my appearance on *Good Morning America.* The station experienced a power failure, so we had to scoot to another. I almost missed my opportunity to explain the split-fingered fastball to the whole country.

Later in the morning I went to our workout at Jack Murphy Stadium and was reminded that it's been five years since the Padres fired me. The security guard wouldn't grant me entrance. "I'm sorry, sir, but unless you have some identification I can't let you in," he politely told me. Eventually another guard recognized me. Walking onto the field, I felt a little nostalgic; I couldn't help but recall the day I was fired. I never experienced mixed emotions over the firing. I always believed I was the man for the job. And I've always felt I managed better in 1979 than in 1978, even though we won sixteen fewer games. Managing is like a roll of the dice. I was able to quickly erase the firing from my mind, partly because I had another job to do as the Tigers pitching coach. I believed everything would work out for the best. It has. Now, I can't think of anything more fitting than coming home and winning the World Series by beating the club that fired me.

Sparky told me he had hoped the Cubs would win the National League pennant. "I knew if you got home it would be tough to get you back," he told me. I don't even want to think about leaving the Tigers.

At the field, I had to cope with the media before practice. All the reporters were asking about the split-fingered fastball. I did a spot for Joe Garagiola of NBC-TV. Our workout was light as we became accustomed to the configurations of the park. Sparky held a lengthy meeting with the players afterward to study scouting reports on the Padres compiled by our special assignment scout Roger Jongewaard. Basically, we decided we would play our third basemen extremely shallow to take the bunt away from Alan Wiggins, and we determined that we would be aggressive offensively.

I retreated to my home later in the day to make sure all my ticket requests were in order. We have a big family! I bought approximately $4,500 worth of tickets for the games in San Diego and another $2,300 worth of tickets for games in Detroit. This is a headache I'd like to have every October.

I needed to relax so I took one of my horses for a short ride. The horse slipped and fell on an asphalt road. I suffered an abrasion on my chin and torn tendons in my right ankle. I was dazed by the fall, but fortunate not to have landed underneath the horse.

The last time I was here I wore a different uniform

TUESDAY, OCTOBER 9   SAN DIEGO

J ACK Morris might qualify as the best opening act in baseball. He got progressively better and went the distance as we defeated the Padres 3-2. Who can dispute the choice of Morris to pitch the big game? He won our season opener against the Minnesota Twins, the opening game of the league Championship Series, and now the first game of the World Series.

In the bullpen before the game I asked Jack how he felt. The crowd was extremely boisterous at this point, as their hometown Padres were being introduced. Jack was absorbing the atmosphere. "You know," he remarked, "this is fun." I headed confidently to the dugout.

Jack had a shaky start, however, and surrendered two runs in the first inning. I'm certain he was a little nervous. He wasn't really cutting loose with his fastball and he guided his split-fingered fastball. I put him in a hole in the third inning by ordering a pitchout twice in a row with Tony Gwynn batting

Larry Herndon came through when we needed him

and Alan Wiggins on first base. Our scouting reports indicated Wiggins prefers to steal on the first or second pitch. He stayed put. I hoped the pitchouts served as a deterrent. Jack walked Gwynn to place runners on first and second with no outs. Steve Garvey was up. I walked to the mound (with my ankle heavily taped to prevent hobbling), and reminded Jack that Garvey would not be bunting and that somewhere in the count we should expect a hit and run. The Padres attempted a hit and run but Garvey bounced into a double play.

Larry Herndon provided Jack with a 3-2 lead by slamming an opposite-field home run in the fifth inning. Sparky suggested that maybe we should allow Jack to pitch seven innings and summon Willie for the last two. I had barely opened my mouth when Sparky looked at me and said, "I know what you're going to say." I said it, anyway. "Let Jack pitch. He's got great stuff."

Morris flaunted that stuff in the sixth inning by striking out Bobby Brown, Carmelo Martinez, and Garry Templeton with two runners on and no outs. "One more runner and we take him out of the game," Sparky said. We didn't have to remove him. In the seventh Jack got quite a break when Kurt Bevacqua tried to stretch a lead-off double into a triple. Bevacqua stumbled slightly rounding second base and was cut down at third on a perfect relay from Kirk Gibson to Lou Whitaker to Marty Castillo. Jack retired the final six batters in order, three on strikes. He finished with nine strikeouts for the game.

There was happiness in the clubhouse, but we realize there's a long way to go. We didn't really swing the bats with authority, probably a sign of nervousness. Jack's performance was the key to this victory. His gritty effort showed me a lot of belly. Of course, he was besieged by the media. I couldn't help but think what the situation might have been if he had maintained his mid-season silence. Instead, he was there to accept credit for his performance. That's the way it should be.

TIGERS 3, PADRES 2   1 – 0

PITCHER	IP	H	R-ER	BB	SO	ERA
Morris (1-0)	9.0	8	2-2	3	9	2.00

WEDNESDAY, OCTOBER 10   SAN DIEGO

TUESDAY'S goat was Wednesday's hero. Kurt Bevacqua didn't worry about stumbling around second base tonight! His three-run homer evened the World Series at one game apiece.

Petry had good stuff but was wild high in the strike zone. He just didn't seem to concentrate as well as I'd like. He was, naturally, chagrined. He didn't care too much for Bevacqua's home run trot, either. Bevacqua did a pirouette before he reached first base and blew kisses to his wife after rounding third base. "I didn't like it," Dan said. "I'll be a different and better pitcher next time."

Sparky and I didn't care much for Bevacqua's antics, either. "I hope all the boys saw it," Sparky said after the game. "I wonder what Milt thought about the kisses?"

At my suggestion, we had sent Wilcox back to Detroit prior to the game. Sparky cleared the move with Jim Campbell and Bill Lajoie. We aren't scheduled to arrive in Detroit until 5:30 A.M. tomorrow. This way Milt can enjoy a solid night's sleep and be adjusted to the time change for his starting assignment in Game 3 on Friday night.

I'm not fretting, but the Padres do have the makings of a good club. We stopped their running game tonight by picking one runner off first and throwing out two others attempting to steal second. But they simply outplayed and outpitched us. Andy Hawkins and Craig Lefferts combined for eight and one-third innings of two-hit pitching in relief. I remember Hawkins as a skinny kid when I managed the Padres. He has blossomed into a hard thrower who comes right at hitters. This was my first look at Lefferts. He has a good fastball that runs away from right-handed hitters and also has a screwball. Both pitchers made our hitters look pretty bad. And if that's not enough, San Diego also has Rich Gossage and Dave Dravecky in a bullpen that might be the best we've encountered all season. Gossage is the only one we have faced before.

I thought after the first inning we had this game wrapped

up. Sparky really took it to Ed Whitson, their starting pitcher. His first three pitches were drilled for line-drive singles and Sparky shifted our running game into high gear. However, that outburst was our only production for the game.

I feel a little twinge of sadness for Berenguer. We had planned to start Juan in Game 4 on Saturday in Detroit had we won the first three games. Those plans have been scrapped; we'll come back with our horse, Morris, on Saturday.

Prior to the game I saw Bob Fontaine, the man most responsible for my firing as San Diego manager. I was on my way to the bullpen when I spotted Fontaine and his wife. We had not seen each other since the day I was relieved of my managerial duties. When I mentioned that to Bob, his wife said, "Oh, Rog, Bob didn't fire you." I didn't say anything.

We used four relief pitchers, including Hernandez. Willie asked if he could pitch one inning, the eighth. Sparky hedged and said, "I don't want him pitching two innings." "Why not?" I said, obviously thinking more optimistically. "If he does, it will mean we've either tied the game or gone ahead." No such luck. We lost 5-3.

We were happy to leave San Diego. Their fans were very vocal and their infield very hard. A ball hit by Terry Kennedy took a bad hop and struck Lou Whitaker in the chest right before Bevacqua connected for his home run—the first we've allowed in eleven games. On the green, green grass of Tiger Stadium, Kennedy's ball probably would have been an inning-ending double play.

We won't hold a workout tomorrow after our four-hour flight home. Rest is more important. I'm going to get as much sleep as possible before greeting a slew of relatives. Three of my brothers have made the trip to Detroit—Charles from New Orleans, Wilson from Durham, and Marvin from Charleston, South Carolina. J.T. is watching from his bed at Duke University Hospital. I anticipate the Tigers will put on a good show for them.

Sparky wasn't happy with the outcome of Game 2

PADRES 5, TIGERS 3   1 – 1

PITCHER	IP	H	R-ER	BB	SO	ERA
Petry (0-1)	4.1	8	5-5	3	2	10.39
Lopez	0.2	1	0-0	1	0	0.00
Scherrer	1.1	2	0-0	0	0	0.00
Bair	0.2	0	0-0	0	1	0.00
Hernandez	1.0	0	0-0	0	0	0.00

W HEN I go back to San Diego I want to relax. No baseball, please. We took a step in that direction tonight by defeating the Padres 5-2.

San Diego pitchers issued eleven walks, which tied a Series record. My good buddy, Norm Sherry, is the pitching coach for the Padres and was a teammate of mine with the Dodgers and Mets. He said you'd expect that kind of performance in a rookie league.

For our part, we left a Series record fourteen runners on the bases tonight. This walkathon lasted three hours and eleven minutes, until nearly midnight. And tomorrow we have a day game! Sparky and I plan to leave for the stadium at 9:30 A.M. This will be a short night. That's just fine with me. I don't like off-days—they take the edge off everything and drag it out.

The pre-game hoopla never ceases to amaze me. I couldn't even watch batting practice from our dugout because of the mass of assembled media. Many continue to ask me about retirement. I will postpone this decision until after the World Series.

Milt allowed one run in six innings to receive credit for the victory. Willie pitched the final two and one-third innings flawlessly. Wilcox struggled with his control early, but found his curve and split-fingered fastball the final three innings he pitched. Sparky thought it was a good idea to remove him after six innings; by then he had thrown 102 pitches. Scherrer relieved Milt and allowed runners to reach second and third base in the seventh before Willie put us in control.

Marty Castillo was our hitting hero tonight. He slammed a two-run home run into the upper deck in left field to trigger a four-run second inning against San Diego starter Tim Lollar. I kidded Marty by saying he should appear on "Good Morning Tijuana." The home run grew in importance because we simply weren't able to capitalize to any extent on the eleven walks. I hope we start hitting soon.

Marty Castillo cracks a two-run home run in our Game 3 victory

I was happy for Marty. He's a delightful person who has accepted his station as a utility player. Before the league Championship Series he told Sparky he was crazy. "I'll show you how crazy I am," responded Sparky. "I'm starting you at third base in the playoffs." "Well, I'll show you how crazy I am," replied Castillo. "I'm going to be the MVP." He certainly was tonight.

I also have to pay tribute to Wilcox. This was a pivotal game. Milt struggled without his best stuff, proving that competitive instincts can overcome other shortcomings. This was his nineteenth victory—seventeen in the regular season, one in the league Championship Series, and one in the World Series. Who would ever have thought in spring training that Wilcox would win nineteen games? Me, that's who!

TIGERS 5, PADRES 2   2 − 1

PITCHER	IP	H	R-ER	BB	SO	ERA
Wilcox (1-0)	6.0	7	1-1	2	4	1.50
Scherrer	0.2	2	1-1	0	0	4.50
Hernandez (S1)	2.1	1	0-0	0	0	0.00

J ACK Morris was to baseball today what Jack Nicklaus can be to golf, Larry Bird to basketball, and John McEnroe to tennis. Jack took charge absolutely. He won his second complete game of the World Series, 4-2, on a pair of two-run home runs by Alan Trammell. A lot of players, coaches, and managers doubted Jack's character during the course of this season. His pitching effectiveness corresponded to his attitude. He pitched extremely well as the carefree Morris we have come to know, and pitched poorly for six weeks when he turned sullen.

Jack certainly has a lot of favorable character witnesses based on his post-season performance—a 3-0 record and five runs in twenty-five innings. This game was the turning point of the Series. We are now up three games to one. We can seal the World Championship here at Tiger Stadium tomorrow.

I've seen and played with some great pitchers—Sandy Koufax, Don Drysdale, Bob Gibson, Don Newcombe, Carl Erskine, and Jim Bunning. None could have done any better than Jack, who gave up five hits and no walks. His only mistake was a slider that Terry Kennedy hit for a home run in the second inning. The other San Diego run scored on a wild pitch

Jack was ready from start to finish in both his Series games

with two outs in the ninth inning. "Who cares!" chanted the zealous Tiger Stadium crowd of 52,130.

Between each inning I asked Jack how he felt. He was working on only three days' rest. "I feel great," he assured me each time I inquired. The only thing tiring him was my question. He finally said, "Don't worry, Rog, I'm going to win this game for us." Jack is a superb athlete in great physical condition who is capable of being in great mental condition when absolutely necessary. He would and could pitch on one or two days' rest in this type of post-season setting.

However, he didn't allow the moment to slip away without a trace of cocky arrogance that often distinguishes great pitchers from good pitchers. He told a large gathering of reporters in our crowded clubhouse following the victory, "Most people believe Babe Ruth was the greatest baseball player ever. I wonder if he could have hit the split-fingered fastball? Ty Cobb? I've seen his swing. I know he couldn't hit it! Maybe they could adjust and be the stars of today. I know there will be teams better than ours. That's the way of the world. Everything gets better." No pitcher got better this season than Morris did.

Following the game, our clubhouse was not boisterous, even though we realize we are on the threshold of a World Championship. We are confident about tomorrow's game. I believe there are a sizeable number of clubs in our division and our league as good as or better than the Padres. I intend to tell that to Petry, tomorrow's starting pitcher.

TIGERS 4, PADRES 2   3 – 1

PITCHER	IP	H	R-ER	BB	SO	ERA
Morris (2-0)	9.0	5	2-2	0	4	2.00

THE clock never struck midnight on our storybook season. What a season! It was like hitting the jackpot on a one-armed bandit. Three ones—111 victories—came up. We ARE the World Champions! We beat the San Diego Padres, 8-4. I am extremely proud—and stunned. Our victory still hasn't sunk in. Everyone wanted to savor the moment. It seemed as if someone always was starting to count us out following our 35-5 start. People said we would fold, but we always snapped back. We didn't dwell on records. Our twenty-five players worked as a unit better than any club I've been associated with.

Alan Trammell was selected the Most Valuable Player of this World Series. Jack Morris was another MVP candidate for his two complete-game victories in a five-game series. I honestly believe the whole team was the MVP, or perhaps Sparky, who welded all the components into a single unit. He wanted to prove to everyone that the Cincinnati Reds made a mistake when they fired him in 1979. He certainly succeeded on that count.

There was an air of confidence in the clubhouse prior to the game. No one planned on returning to San Diego.

Kirk Gibson was an offensive cloudburst. The thunder came in the form of two home runs to account for five runs, the lightning on a dash home from third base. He tagged up and scored on a sacrifice fly to second baseman Alan Wiggins and broke a 3-3 tie in the fifth inning to put us ahead for keeps. Third base coach Alex Grammas had Kirk tag up on Rusty Kuntz's short pop to right field. Alex said, "Go, go!" but Gibby thought he said, "No, no." Gibby was going anyway. That's his aggressive nature. His second home run of the game was struck off Goose Gossage in the eighth inning. Suddenly our precarious 5-4 lead jumped to 8-4. I'll never forget Gibby jumping into the air following this home run. It was as if he was saying to the world, "Here we are, the World Champions."

San Diego manager Dick Williams wanted to walk Kirk intentionally. He signalled that to catcher Terry Kennedy but

Series MVP Alan Trammell   *Kirk Gibson celebrates*

Gossage disagreed. Williams went to the mound and I guess Gossage changed Dick's mind. Now Dick is faced with a lot of second-guessers. I feel sorry for him. He's a fine manager who did an outstanding job advancing the Padres to the World Series, where there is no shame in losing.

Dick knows in his heart he wanted to walk Gibson. He would have preferred to pitch to Parrish, even though Lance hit a home run off the Goose in the previous inning. Lance is not fleet afoot so a walk to Gibson would have allowed the infield to play at its normal depth. A double play would then have been in order.

Petry started but met the same fate as in Game 2: he couldn't get ahead in the count. Sparky removed Dan in the fourth inning with the game tied 3-3. Scherrer pitched one inning before being replaced by Lopez, who blew smoke right past the Padres. Aurelio struck out four of the seven batters he faced. He was emotionally high and had great control of his fastball—twenty-one of his twenty-five pitches were strikes. Sparky decided to use Hernandez for the final two innings. I'm sure some fans raised their eyebrows, but you go with your best in that situation. The Padres had Graig Nettles and Kennedy as their first two hitters in the eighth inning. Both swing from the left side and neither was going to be removed for a pinch-hitter.

Willie did execute one key pickoff play with the score standing in our favor at 5-4 in the eighth inning. Luis Salazar was on first base as the potential tying run with two outs. Normally, a runner will not attempt to steal in this situation. I wanted to make sure. I signalled for Willie to throw to first base. Salazar was leaning toward second base, so I had Willie throw over again. So long, Salazar. So long, San Diego.

Willie retired Tony Gwynn on a fly ball to left fielder Larry Herndon for the final out of the game, preserving a remarkable statistic: a 98-0 record in games in which we led in the ninth inning. What a bullpen!

Pandemonium struck when Gwynn's fly ball nestled into Herndon's glove. In the dugout, we shoved our caps into our shirts so they couldn't be stolen. Willie drew everyone to him as if he were a magnet. We pressed together so tightly that Willie swallowed his plug of chewing tobacco and was sick to his stomach in the clubhouse. I spotted Bill Lajoie and congratulated him on a fine job of assembling this team. "Does this mean we've got a deal?" he asked. I didn't commit myself. The final decision will be made more easily at home.

I did a guest spot on a television show—*Night Watch* on CBS—with Tommy Lasorda a few hours after the game. The network sent two limousines for Carolyn, me, and eleven members of our family. Afterward, we went back to our condominium for champagne. I could become an alcoholic with all the champagne we've had this year!

Carolyn and I telephoned all four of our children. This is my fourth World Series ring—one for each child. This one goes to our youngest daughter, Vikki, who's not much of a baseball fan and wants me to keep the ring. It's yours, darling.

I felt all along we would win the World Series easily. The biggest hurdle was getting through the league Championship Series. I think baseball should do something about that format, although I can't offer any solutions. It just doesn't seem fair that our club, which won 104 games, should have had to beat

Petry keeps getting better

Lopez smoked 'em for the win

*Willie got the final out
in each of our clinchers*

*Owner Tom Monaghan
celebrates with us*

the Kansas City Royals, winners of only 84 games, in a best-of-five shootout. That was pressure. A lot of people would've said we choked if we'd lost.

I was a pitcher for the World Champion Brooklyn Dodgers my first season in the major leagues in 1955 and now served as pitching coach of the World Champion Tigers in what probably will be my final season in 1984. What more can a man ask for?

TIGERS 8, PADRES 4   4 − 1

PITCHER	IP	H	R-ER	BB	SO	ERA
Petry	3.2	6	3-3	2	2	9.00
Scherrer	1.0	1	0-0	0	0	3.00
Lopez (1-0)	2.1	0	0-0	0	4	0.00
Hernandez (S2)	2.0	3	1-1	0	0	1.69

WORLD SERIES STATISTICS

PITCHER	G	GS	W-L	Saves	IP	H	R-ER	ERA	BB	SO
Morris	2	2	2-0	0	18.0	13	4-4	2.00	3	13
Petry	2	2	0-1	0	8.0	14	8-8	9.00	5	4
Wilcox	1	1	1-0	0	6.0	7	1-1	1.50	2	4
Bair	1	0	0-0	0	0.2	0	0-0	0.00	0	1
Scherrer	3	0	0-0	0	3.0	5	1-1	3.00	0	0
Lopez	2	0	1-0	0	3.0	1	0-0	0.00	1	4
Hernandez	3	0	0-0	2	5.1	4	1-1	1.69	0	0
Totals	14	5	4-1	2	44.0	44	15-15	3.07	11	26

CUMULATIVE POST-SEASON STATISTICS

PITCHER	G	GS	W-L	Saves	IP	H	R-ER	ERA	BB	SO
Bair	1	0	0-0	0	0.2	0	0-0	0.00	0	1
Hernandez	6	0	0-0	3	9.1	7	2-2	1.93	1	3
Lopez	3	0	2-0	0	6.0	5	0-0	0.00	2	6
Morris	3	3	3-0	0	25.0	18	5-5	1.80	4	17
Petry	3	3	0-1	0	15.0	18	10-10	6.00	6	8
Scherrer	3	0	0-0	0	3.0	5	1-1	3.00	0	0
Wilcox	2	2	2-0	0	14.0	9	1-1	0.64	4	12
Totals	21	8	7-1	3	73.0	62	19-19	2.34	17	47

EPILOGUE

ROGER and Carolyn drove to San Diego a few days after the Series. Dan Petry headed for Myrtle Beach, South Carolina, to vacation with his wife, Chris. Jack Morris was off for his annual hunting expedition in Montana. Doug Bair returned to his home in Loveland, Ohio. Willie Hernandez, winner of the 1984 Cy Young award, left for Aguada, Puerto Rico, and Aurelio Lopez for Tecamachalco, Mexico. Dave Rozema, Milt Wilcox, and Juan Berenguer remained in the Detroit area.

The team's "reunion" won't come until February 1985 in Lakeland, Florida, where the crowds are small and the World Series is history. These players and coaches may never be reunited as a group. Whether the same pitchers or Roger Craig himself is back in Tigers stripes next year is a story for next season. The stories of *this* season are over and written. Thanks to Roger for once again putting 'em down in order.